As One of Them

As One of Them

LETTERS TO A SISTER SUPERIOR

by Claude Kean, O.F.M.

Have they made thee ruler? Be not lifted up:
be among them as one of them (Ecclus. 32:1).

THE NEWMAN PRESS • 1965 • WESTMINSTER, MD.

First published May, 1965
Second printing January, 1966

Imprimi Potest: DONALD HOAG, O.F.M.
Minister Provincial

Nihil Obstat: REV. WILLIAM J. KING, S.T.D.
Censor Librorum

Imprimatur: MOST REV. JAMES J. NAVAGH, D.D.
Bishop of Paterson
March 26, 1965

 Library of Congress Catalog Card Number: 64-66335. Printed in the United States of America.

Contents

As One of Them

1. "*I Have Appointed Thee*"

Dear Sister,

Between the lines of your letter, I hear a telegrapher's key clicking out an S.O.S. Without forewarning, you find yourself Superior of Saint Anselm's Convent and Principal of Saint Anselm's School. You turn, distraught, to your aging uncle and ask in effect, "What must I do to be saved?" Well, though devoid of ideas on most subjects, I do happen to have a few ideas on Superiorship: several of them distilled from experience with it, more of them from reading about it, most of them from observation of it during forty-some years of religious life. You shall have those ideas, whatever their worth. May they light a candle or two in your "encircling gloom"!

First of all, I'm genuinely pleased that you think yourself unworthy of Superiorship. ("Mother must have confused me, Sister Clare, with Sister Clarissa.") That sort of humility is a good omen. For it is a truism that the only ones fit to be Superiors are those that doubt they are. Only such know their limitations and their need of assistance. Only such will be "not lifted up," but will live and work among their subjects "as one of them."

Should you, you ask, have declined your appointment? Yes and no. Yes, if you played politics to get it. Your Superiorship would then be the fulfillment of your own will, not of the Will of God. (Proving the human side of the Church, Superiorship *is* occasionally won through political maneuvers, to the detriment of all.) But you did not seek Superiorship. You had not the most anemic aspiration towards it. So in your case the answer is, No. Your acceptance of Superiorship is simply a matter of obedience. The grace of God is in it, because the Will of God is in it. To oppose His Will would be patently wrong.

But, you demur, you are so relatively young to be a Superior. ("One of my subjects, Sister Martin, was my Mistress of Novices; another, Sister Eleanor, was my Superior at Holy Rosary.") So what? Seniority may determine the appointments of diocesan priests to pastorates; it has nothing to do with the appointments of religious to Superiorships. Saint Francis of Assisi declared he would gladly obey a novice recently admitted to the novitiate, if that novice were appointed his Superior. You will, I grant, be a younger Superior than the average. But so was the bishop Timothy, to whom Saint Paul wrote: "Let no man despise thy youth" (I Tim. 4:12). You have at least the age required by your Constitutions. That's all that matters.

You further protest that your future subjects are so much holier than you ("Sister Thomasine is a living saint!"), and so much brighter than you ("Sister Edmunda holds three degrees!"), and so much more personable ("Everybody *loves* Sister Maurice!"), that any of them would make a much better Superior than you will make. I should be uneasy if you thought otherwise: if you thought that on all these three counts *you* were the logical choice for Superiorship, and wired congratulations to Mother Provincial for her perspicacity in having named you. With such amazingly fine people as your subjects, your term of office ought to be a joyous sinecure.

But what's this holier-than-I business? Since when is an appointment to Superiorship a canonization, or even a beatification? You may be, for all I know, "a little less than the angels." So, considerably less, were the Jewish ecclesiastical rulers in the time of Christ, the Scribes and the Pharisees who sat "in the chair of Moses." Yet Christ charged His disciples: "All things therefore whatsoever they shall say to you, observe and do . . ." (Matt. 23:2). Even if you are no saint, Superiorship can make a saint of you in a hurry, if you let it. That, in fact, is its divinely ordained purpose in your regard. Previously your religious perfection lay in striving to be a good subject; when you assume office, it will lie in striving to be a good Superior.

And this brighter-than-I business? Maybe some *are* brighter. But since when is Superiorship a medal for the highest I. Q. in a religious community? The Apostles, Superiors all, were no Ph. D.'s. Our Lord's simplest parables went over their heads. As to executive ability, probably the only one of them who knew anything at all about book-keeping and accounting was Matthew, the former tax-collector. Do you know what Saint Teresa of Avila prized most highly in a Superior? Not piety nor learning, but common sense. She explains in that wonderfully forthright way of hers: "A devout nun, if she has no brains, is of use only to herself. But I can put a sensible nun at the head of the house and trust her with any of the offices." Without avuncular partiality, I believe you can easily pass this Teresian test.

And this more-personable-than-I business? Since when is Superiorship a blue ribbon awarded to the winner in a popularity contest? Of course, if there's a heavy debt on the new motherhouse or the new academy, a Superior *might* be appointed solely for her golden personality, her ability to win lay friends and influence lay people. But if her charge is the more normal task of fostering the holiness and happiness of her subjects, she needs no phenomenal personality-rating. She needs only a cool head and a warm heart.

Well, then, if your Superiorship doesn't depend on your sanctity or learning or personality or on the absence of them, on what then does it depend? Entirely on the authority conferred upon you. This point is of such pivotal importance that I'll devote my next letter entirely to it. For the present, remember that your Superiorship is equated with authority; and that, as Our Lord reminded Pilate, and as Saint Paul reminded all Christians, all authority is of God. "I have appointed thee," God tells you as distinctly as He told Moses of old. You are to represent Him among your subjects. You are to be His ambassador with portfolio, commissioned and empowered to negotiate the affairs of your Sovereign. "He who hears you," He declares, "hears Me: and he who despises you despises Me." Why, therefore, should you fear to assume office? God has appointed you, and God will assist you to fulfill your appointment if you do not block His way.

You realize, I presume, that Superiorship will effect overnight some drastic and disturbing changes in your *modus vivendi*. What changes? Here are some that come to mind. The list is imposing.

First, you might as well remove your door from its hinges and install in its place a revolving door. For your subjects will converge on your room at all hours with queries, proposals, requests, critiques. All the time, your time will be their time.

Secondly, till now you have always stood comfortably in the background, one of the blurred many. Now you will stand in painful pre-eminence, with kleig lights glaring on you. Your every word will be parsed, your every motive sifted, your every move noted, your every fault and failing catalogued. The "giftie" that Bobby Burns sighed for—"to see ourselves as others see us"—will indeed be yours, in king-sized form. You'll inhabit a house of mirrors.

Thirdly, from a relatively care-free existence you will enter upon an inescapably care-fretted one. The spiralling cost of living (and, perhaps, of dying), the many and various needs of the members of a community, the intricacies of bookkeeping and budget-balancing, the special tact required in dealing with each of your subjects, the preservation of the communal peace, the myriad details involved in the maintenance of a building, the persistence of insurance agents and candle salesmen, the vagaries of gardeners and janitors and roofers and painters and plumbers—of such troublesome matters, and of a hundred others like them, you'll soon acquire first-hand knowledge. You'll suspect that, by comparison, Atlas was a man with an hallucination: his mighty muscles straining under a burden that was in reality nothing but an oversized blue bubble.

Fourthly, from a mind-my-own-business private citizen, you'll become of necessity a mind-everybody's-business public official, the protector and corrector of your community. As protector, you'll be a lightning rod, the target of all criticism directed against your community. As corrector, you'll learn, with the Gilbert and Sullivan cops, that

> When constabulary duty's to be done,
> A policeman's lot is not a happy one.

The conclusion? Someone, undoubtedly a Superior, expressed it well: "There is only one thing worse than being a subject: and that is, having a subject." A layman rejoices when he's promoted to head his department or his firm; for the promotion bolsters his pride and his purse. But a knowledgeable religious counts her promotion to Superiorship not a signal honor, but a signal onus.

Yet, obviously, there must be Superiors. In their salad days, the Soviets set up a directorless symphony orchestra. ("Directors belong to decadent capitalism!") With nobody authorized to decide what the orchestra would play and how they would play it, the experiment was an immediate and monumental failure. Grudgingly, they simply had to put somebody on a podium with a baton in his hand. No less necessary is a director or Superior in a religious community. Saint Bonaventure—you'd do well, by the way, to read his *Six Wings of the Seraphim,* a classic on Superiorship—says that religious need Superiors for four reasons: 1) to teach them in the school of Christ; 2) to exercise them in good works; 3) to guard them from sin; 4) to correct them. It would not tax the mind to add at least fourteen more, though lesser, reasons to these four.

Is it any wonder, then, that Saint Gregory Nazianzen calls Superiorship "the art of arts, the science of sciences"? Or any wonder that Saint Paul asks prayers for all "in high places"? Those heights can be so terribly exposed and cold and lonely and dizzy. They can do strange things to men, making saints of some and sinners of others. I'll take my cue from Saint Paul and pray for my newly elevated niece, "without ceasing" (Thess. I: 5:17).

Your affectionate uncle,

FATHER C.

2. *"There is no Power but from God"*

Dear Sister,

Years ago a brash, gum-chewing, fast-talking young Brother arrived at his newly assigned friary and reported to his Father Guardian. The Guardian, a gray, gaunt man known for his ascetic ways, briefed the new arrival: "I expect you, Brother, to obey not only my explicit commands, but my implicit wishes."

"Huh," snorted the Brother, "you expect divination. That's against the First Commandment!"

Unperturbed, the Guardian continued: "As Superior, you know, I have a spark of the divine in me."

"A spark!" countered the Brother. "I'm in the state of grace, so I've got the Blessed Trinity in me!"

Quick curtain. . . . What the Guardian tried to say, without quite succeeding, was simply this: "As Superior, I have authority from God."

When you think of it, authority, in its inner workings, is something of a mystery, isn't it? That all men are created equal is more than a noble American slogan; it's a theological verity. There is no "super-race," there are no "super-men." All men come into this world with the same basic, inalienable human rights. So from where does one man draw the right to rule over another? Saint Paul, echoing Christ's words to Pilate, answers: "There is no power but from God: and those that are, are ordained of God" (Rom. 13:1).

The word "authority" derives, as you know, from the word "author." And the dictionary defines an author as "an originator, first cause, creator." God is the Author, the Creator, of all men. Authority over them is exclusively His prerogative. He alone may rightfully tell them, "Thou shalt," and, "Thou shalt not." But in His government of men, God has delegated certain aspects of His authority to human beings: to parents, authority over their children; to bishops, authority "to rule the Church of God" (Acts 20:28); to civil rulers, authority to conduct affairs of state. God has made this authority inherent in some human roles, such as parenthood. In other roles, He has made the authority to stem from the free will of those governed. The authority of a pope, for instance, initially accrues to him from the freely cast ballots of cardinal electors; of a president or a governor or a mayor, from the freely cast ballots of citizens.

For the sake of greater efficiency in ruling, those in authority may subdelegate their authority in part to others: as parents do to teachers, popes to cardinals, and presidents to cabinet members and ambassadors. But in all its ramifications, all authority stems back to the Author, to God; all authority including the authority of Superiors in religious life. The Major Superior gets his or her authority from the votes of the electors. He or she then delegates certain aspects of that authority to the local Superiors. And that, dear Sister, is how you got *your* badge. It may seem a bit tarnished or second-hand, but on the back it's still clearly stamped *Made in Heaven.*

I wonder, has it ever struck you as odd that people refer to an office of authority as a "chair"? For instance, the Chair of Moses, the Chair of Peter, a Chair of Philosophy or of Literature, "the Chair recognizes . . . ." Why not call it a desk, or a podium, or a lectern? Did whoever introduced the "chair" mean to hint cynically that most incumbents in office have nothing to do but sit down and doze? That's a question for philologists to answer. Personally, I rather suspect that many of those chairs, at least in religious circles, prove to be not easy chairs, but electric chairs. Nevertheless, a chair does symbolize an office; and once a religious wag, conscious of this symbolism, described the elections in his community in these words: "Some moved from floor to chair, some from chair to floor, some from chair to chair, and some from floor to floor." Mark well the difference between moving *to* a chair and moving *from* it: the mover-to acquires the authority of an office; the mover-from loses that authority. Significantly, the latter is termed an "ex."

Why belabor so obvious a point? Because to some religious it's not at all obvious. Once they were Superiors, but they forget they're Superiors no longer. With what result? A newly installed Father Guardian asked the Brother refectorian to remove from the refectory tables their old oilcloth covering, which offended both the eye and the nose. The Brother obeyed. The next morning, though, the Guardian found the oilcloth back on the tables.

"Why?" he asked.

With a shrug of the shoulders, the Brother answered, "Your predecessor told me to put it back."

Would it be surprising if that poor Brother developed schizophrenia?

Today, as I write, we have on the American scene three ex-Presidents, Hoover, Truman, and Eisenhower. Suppose that, forgetting their *ex* status, all three of them began to issue presidential orders: that Hoover, on Monday, launched a National Food Austerity Program; that Truman, on Tuesday, decreed the disbanding of the Peace Corps; that Eisenhower, on Wednesday, ordered the immediate invasion of Castro's Cuba. If these three were to forget their lack of presidential authority, it is theoretically possible that some of their ardent old camp-followers too might forget it and rally round their heroes' flags. Meanwhile, Lyndon B. Johnson, the man currently in the presidential chair, would be issuing clear and loud counterorders. The Tower of Babel would be with us again, with all its clamor, conflict, and chaos. Well, dear Sister, echoes of Babel are sure to bounce around in any convent where ex-Superiors try to exercise the authority of which they have been dispossessed. For the preservation of the general sanity, the one *in* the chair must politely but firmly remind them that they are *out* of the chair. It's as simple as that.

You know full well that your authority is not absolute, not "all power in heaven and on earth." It has definite fences around it. It is restricted, first, by the laws of God. I think I hear you protest, "I would never knowingly command any of my subjects to break the least of those laws!" I'm sure you would never: never urge any of your subjects to steal or lie or disobey higher authorities or miss Mass on Sunday or eat meat on Friday, or do any other obvious wrong. But I trust I'm not impertinent in warning you against wrongs that are not always so obvious: against Solomon's "little foxes" that can sneak into the vineyard under cover of darkness and "destroy the grapevines" (Cant. 2:15). For instance, see that you never, out of a love of poverty, reach into any school funds for convent needs; never, out of that same love, ask a Sister to mimeograph copyrighted plays or music, thus depriving the authors of their just royalties; never, to avoid unhappy repercussions from diocesan school authorities, permit a Sister to raise her pupils' examination marks unwarrantedly; never, for the love of dear old Saint Anselm's, look the other way while the basketball coach uses players ineligible according to diocesan rules. On and on the list could go: "little foxes" all such offences, but foxes nevertheless. To scent them, you have to be a watchdog always on the prowl.

Secondly, the scope of your authority is restricted by the laws of the Church. To cite several examples: you may not, according to Church law, demand that your Sisters approach the Communion rail in the order of their seniority (you know, wheel-chairs first); you may not demand of them a manifestation of their consciences (Leo XIII scotched that one); you may not deny them permission to consult a confessor other than the appointed confessor of the convent (he too might relish the change). It is essential that you know what Canon Law says a Superior may or may not do. Any one of numerous books on this matter will enlighten you.

Thirdly, the range of your authority is defined by your Rule, your Constitutions, your Book of Customs. All of them say, "So far shalt thou go, and no farther." Your Sisters are not Poor Clares—so you're not entitled to make them walk about barefoot, no matter how picturesque you might consider that custom. They are not Trappestines—so you may not enjoin perpetual silence on them, even though you might be convinced it would do them a world of good. They vowed to observe the Rule of your particular Institute; that is the only Rule you may direct them to observe. "So far—no farther." In this outsider's lowly opinion, the "so far" of your Rule, with its many and minute "Do's" and "Don'ts," is quite far enough. It can make your community a community of saints.

After all this talk about authority, it's high time we asked, What *is* authority? Well, for one answer, it's not infallibility. That, you know, is a much limited and little exercised papal prerogative. In a private audience with Pope John XXIII, Cardinal Cushing, in reply to the Pope's inquiry about his health, admitted that he suffered considerably from a stomach ulcer. Pope John recommended bicarbonate of soda. With a wry smile, Cardinal Cushing answered: "I'm afraid Your Holiness' infallibility isn't up to par to-day. Bicarbonate of soda is about the worst thing possible to feed an ulcer." Don't be distressed if you, a Superior considerably less than a pope, can make occasional mistakes. You can appoint subjects to the wrong tasks. You can grant permissions that might better have been withheld and vice versa. You can formulate policies that, objectively viewed, are less than Solomonic in wisdom. You can misread the innocence or the guilt of subjects. You can make vast purchases of under-priced paint or laundry soap or floor wax that the Better Business Bureau, if consulted, would have warned you against buying. No, you are not infallible; so please never think and speak and act as though you are! But—the irony of it!—your subjects *are* infallible. I mean, you may err in commanding them, but they cannot err in obeying you. Scripture says so: "An obedient man shall speak of victory" (Prov. 21:28). Well, don't fret over the disparity between their lot and yours. So long as your mistakes are honest mistakes, are mistakes of the head and not of the heart, you'll merit even by your blundering.

No, authority is not infallibility. Nor is it a purely personal boon, like a fortune left by a rich aunt to her favorite niece. It exists not for the benefit of the one possessing it, but for the benefit of his or her subjects. Almost any time I scan the newspapers, I'm appalled at the reported misuse of power in the world of politics. I read of senators and congressmen who put their wives, sons, and daughters on the public payroll as vague "secretaries" or "assistants"; who embark on round-the-world, government-paid junkets to make mysterious ethnological "studies" for reports to Congress at some uncertain future date. I read of mayors and councilmen and borough managers and commissioners who begin their regimes by unanimously voting themselves fat increases in salaries, and continue their regimes by collecting under-the-table fees for concessions, considerations, or contracts. But what appalls me most is that, if these public stewards are called to account before some committee of investigation, all of them blandly profess to see no "irregularity" in any of their Machiavelian maneuvers. To them, office means not responsibilities to the public, but opportunities for themselves; not public service, but self-service.

Resolve, I beg you, that your office will never mean to you anything even remotely like that. Resolve that you will never use it as a ticket to gracious living. You will not, if you follow this rule: *Allow yourself as Superior no privilege you would not allow to any and all of your subjects.* That means, no special room furnishings, no special menu, no special funds to use on yourself, no special pleasure trips, no special vacations, no special exemptions from the common life and labors. Be ever "among them as one of them," and they will respect you and love you and obey you.

At long last, having said what authority is not, I'm ready to say what it is. It is the moral power to direct another to his rightful goal. I want you to look long at that definition, to mull it over. For it'll be the theme of my next letter. We'll see what happens when we preface the word "authority" with the word "religious." The results may mildly surprise you.

Your affectionate uncle,

FATHER C.

3. *"Take and Read"*

Dear Sister,

The moral power to direct another to his rightful goal—that's authority, remember? That's what it means in the home, the school, the city, the state, and the nation. And that's what it means in the Church.

As a Newman Club Chaplain at a state university some years ago, I was occasionally invited to address one or the other Protestant student group on the campus; to tell them, as they rather naïvely phrased their invitations, "something about the Catholic Church." Well, one "something" I always told them was, that the Catholic Church is strong on authority. She unabashedly claims authority, said I; she unabashedly exercises it. (Studious contraction of brows.) She articulately and emphatically tells her members what they must think, believe, and do. No "if's" and "but's" about it. (Robin-like cocking of heads.) Quite understandably, Protestants take a dim view of this dictatorial spirit of the Catholic Church. They cherish their personal freedom of belief and practice—their freedom, as one minister has proudly described it, "even to be wrong." (Hurrah-for-us smiles.) All right, then, let them enjoy their freedom. But we Catholics, so frightfully conscious of our human ignorance and fallibility, prefer to have the Church, a learned, experienced and enlightened teacher, tell us what's what, instead of trying to figure it out by ourselves. (Slow pursing of lips.) We gladly surrender liberty of thought, to gain insurance against error. We gladly abdicate petty autonomy, to obtain sovereign security. Losing our lives, we find them. (No cheers, but a few thoughtful expressions.)

Now, authority in religious life is merely the authority of the Church brought into particular focus; authority centered upon the goal of religious life, namely, religious perfection. How is that goal to be reached? Primarily through the observance of the religious Rule and Constitutions. So the authority of a religious Superior is the authority to direct his or her religious subjects towards religious perfection by helping them to observe their Rule and Constitutions. That is the Superior's raison d'être. As surely as the subjects are called to perfection, so surely must the Superior see to it that they answer this call.

A priest whom I know was appointed dean of discipline in a Catholic college for men. The appointment really stunned him; he knew next to nothing about this difficult phase of college administration. But at the first assembly of the school year, he held aloft in view of the student-body a small blue book containing the traditional disciplinary rules of the college. "Thanks be to God for this!" he said. "Everything that both you and I need to know about the college discipline is here in this little book. Fortunately you can read and I can read. And that's all we have to do to get along famously together, just read and follow this little blue book. And by the way," he added, "though the little book's blue, it wasn't designed to make little boys blue. Just the opposite. It was designed to keep little boys from getting blue, by helping them accomplish what they came here for." Well, like that priest, you have been appointed to a new and difficult role. You are more fortunate, though, than he: you have not merely one book, but three books, to assist and guide you: your Rule, your Constitutions, and your Book of Customs. They tell you every jot and tittle of what you must know and do. And like the little blue book, their purpose is to help, not to hinder. So I urge you, as a mysterious voice urged Saint Augustine, "Take and read." Those books, you know, can cover much of your beginner's inadequacy, as a good syllabus can cover much of the inadequacy of a young, uncertain teacher.

To return to the main motif of this letter, your top-drawer obligation as Superior is to maintain the religious life and discipline of your convent. For this reason your Major Superior appointed you, trusting in your common sense and your sense of responsibility. Come to think of it, your commission has much in common with that of the policeman who patrols the neighborhood, hasn't it? He represents civic law and order on his assigned beat; you represent religious law and order in your assigned convent. His job is to see that the people in his area behave like good citizens; yours is to see that the people in your convent behave like good religious. He didn't make the laws he must enforce, nor did you make yours. Hence he's not free, out of big-heartedness, to ignore them, much less to repeal them; neither are you. If he neglects his job by absenting himself from it (conversing with bar-tenders in taverns on his beat, or playing pinochle with the boys at the local fire station) or if he benevolently closes his eyes to all sorts of wrong-doing along his beat, his area may turn into a jungle where nobody can walk safely. If you neglect your job, well, I need not spell out the harm, even the disaster, that can befall your convent. With such close kinship to him, don't you feel like inviting him into the convent for coffee and doughnuts and a tête-a-tête the next time he strolls into sight?

Bear with me if, in a negative way, I compare your role to that of another type of official, a college sorority house mother. You're not acquainted with the lady? Then I'll introduce you. She's usually a sweet, genteel, silverhaired little lady who inhabits a modest apartment on the first floor of the sorority house. She's there to fulfill a catalogue requirement comforting to parents: "Every sorority house shall have a resident sorority 'mother,' a woman of maturity and excellent reputation, who shall," and so on. Her chief duty, as O. Henry said of an old Indian nurse, is to see that time goes by without skipping a cog. Most of the day she sits in her chintzed and cretonned boudoir, crocheting, writing letters, reading novels, or watching television. At dinner, over which she graciously presides, she calls all her girls "dear"—"Betty, dear," "Eloise, dear," and all the rest. Her most ingratiating charm is her discreetness. Though not afflicted pathologically by temporary losses of sight or hearing or speech, she can always be counted on not to see or hear or say anything the girls would rather she didn't. And she has a cannily delicate instinct for knowing just when to go downtown to the movies, so that her girls may entertain their fraternity boy-friends without the awkward restraint her oldish presence might impose on them. All her girls, of course, positively adore her.

"Just a minute!" I hear you say. "Are you suggesting there are any convent Superiors like *her?*" No, not entirely like her—at least not in their attitude towards gentlemen visitors. But like her, yes, in many other respects. Like her in their donothingness. Like her in their quest for popularity among their subjects. Like her in their absenteeism, their shirking of responsibilities, their condoning of irregularities. One such Superior's motto is avowedly, "Keep everybody happy." In itself, surely, that's a worthy motto, much better than, "Keep everybody miserable." But it's not worthy in this Superior's interpretation of it: "Keep them happy by letting them alone, letting them do whatever they want." I suspect that Superior really means: "Let *me* alone; do not disturb me." If asked to give reasons for this let-them-alone policy, this Superior answers, "My subjects are all adults. All have consciences. All know their obligations, and all will fulfill them." Just like that!

Unfortunately, though, it's not just like that. "Let them alone." Do you know what Solomon, a man experienced and inspired, says of this sort of neglectful supervision? "The child that is left to his own will bring his mother to shame" (Prov. 29:15). If for "the child" we substitute "the religious" (both, after all, are by obedience bound to follow the judgment and will of superiors, who in turn are bound to direct them), the truth of the text holds: "The religious that is left to her own will bring her mother—her community, her Church—to shame." Is this not the short-hand story of many a lost religious vocation? The religious, beginning plainly to neglect religious life, was left to her own. No Superior took her aside, called attention to her irregularities. She was left alone, and alone she went on—and eventually she went off. Do you wonder that Our Lord, in the Apocalypse, lashed with reproach the bishops of Pergamus and Thyatira for sleepily tolerating abuses among their subjects, and that He warned those bishops to wake up before divine punishment overtook them?

Let's come back to you and yours. It ought, surely, to be self-evident that, had your Sisters wanted to be left to themselves, they would have stayed in the world, where most adults have at least some measure of self-rule. Or they would have gone off alone to some desert or some hillside cave. They would never, in their right minds, have come to a convent. They would never have knelt down and vowed obedience to somebody else, putting the running of their lives completely under somebody else's supervision. Out the window, then, with this let-them-alone theory!

Out, too, with the reasons alleged for it. "They are adults." No question about that. It is even a kindly understatement about the jubilarians. "They know their obligations." No question about that either. After the novitiate training, the meditations, the spiritual reading, the monthly conferences and the yearly retreats, how could they help but know them?" "Therefore they will fulfill their obligations." What an unwarrantedly optimistic conclusion! Don't the weekly confessions of religious testify, with clamant clarity, to the difference between knowing obligations and fulfilling them? It would be grand if, just as a dog instinctively goes out (so the philosophers phrase it) to a bone, a religious instinctively went out to a *bonum*. It would be grand if, just as a sunflower naturally turns toward the sun, with no gardener's hand needed to coax it, a religious naturally turned toward God's Will, without encouragement or aid. But fallen human nature doesn't work that way. "Man is prone to evil from his youth," says Scripture—to evil, not to good. He needs a hand to help him towards good, even at times to push him. So do not, dear Sister, keep your hand modestly in your sleeve all the time.

During Benediction one evening in a preparatory seminary for boys, I was struck by the dismally low pitch of the little reed organ. (You may remember, I used to play the organ a bit myself.) Afterwards, the Brother organist explained that he had purposely tuned the organ down two notes, to accommodate it to the changing voices of the growing boys. I wondered to myself why, instead of lowering the pitch of the organ, he hadn't tried to raise the pitch of the voices. Maybe there's a lesson here for you, a Superior. You may not tune down your Rule to accommodate it to the convenience of your subjects, or to the low standards of the times. You must, rather, try to raise your subject's performance to the perfect pitch of your Rule. The tuning-down tendency is an ancient one. Saint Bonaventure noted it almost seven centuries ago, and decried it. "A country," he wrote, "is better without religious at all, if they cannot or will not live therein as religious; for then there is no fear of either their perishing themselves or of giving scandal to others." Saint Teresa apparently had this same thought in mind when she urged parents: "Marry off your daughters, rather than send them to a lax convent!" No down-tuner was Teresa!

When assigned to my first retreat for religious Superiors several years ago, I asked an aged religious priest, a man of holiness and wisdom, what I should stress. He answered unhesitatingly: "Stress that a Superior's first duty is to keep the daily schedule intact, and to insist on regular attendance at the religious exercises. Saint Paul, you know, charges the Superior to 'rule well his household,' and there can be no ruling well without maintaining order and regularity. Rarely should the Superior permit subjects to deviate from the schedule. Certainly not for the sake of visitors, school play rehearsals, shopping, or writing a thesis. Only for a rare and grave reason. Of course, the Superior herself should not change the schedule capriciously. If she 'plays it by ear,' frequently altering the horarium, soon nobody knows what to expect; and the poor, confused Sisters go around asking one another, 'What time is Office?' or, 'What time do we get up to-morrow?' The Superior, I repeat, should keep the daily schedule intact. Few things less than a fire or a flood, or an earthquake should prompt her to change it."

Father's mention of fire recalled an incident that occurred when one of our largest friaries was aflame on a May afternoon in 1930. The fire started at about three-thirty. Because the building was old and lacked all fire-proofing, it burned fast and furiously. By five o'clock it was an inferno with flames leaping through it in an orgy, walls crashing down, smoke rolling off it in great clouds. At five-fifteen an octogenarian friar, renowned for his strict observance of the schedule, came with his biscuit-sized watch in his hand to the Guardian, who stood on the lawn watching the debacle, and asked, "Father Guardian, where do we chant Matins and Lauds?" Seemingly, the old friar wanted to vie with Sidrach, Misach, and Abdenago, the young men who, in the fiery furnace lit by Nabuchodonosor's fury, "walked in the midst of the flame, praising God and blessing the Lord" (Daniel 3:24). Though his judgment was on this occasion questionable, his zeal for the regular observance was commendable.

One more observation and I'm through with the topic of authority. The religious discipline maintained by the Superior must be maintained also by the Assistant in the Superior's absence. Authority has been given to both of them for that self-same purpose. There must be no "house divided," with the Superior symbolizing Justice and the Assistant symbolizing Mercy, the latter calling off all discipline as soon as the former leaves the convent. The slogan of the Assistant must be, "Business as usual."

Your affectionate uncle,

FATHER C.

4. *"To Everyone a Penny"*

Dear Sister,

So it has come to pass: from Sister you have evolved into Sister Superior. What you term your "debut" occurred last Sunday afternoon, when the former Superior vacated the "chair" and you sat down in it. Well, I wish you happy sitting —a blessed tenure of office. May your joys be many and your sorrows few!

It was good to hear of the surprise party the Sisters gave you Sunday evening, with the welcome address, the spiritual bouquet, the clever skit about Superiorship, the home-made version of "Don't Fence Me (Us) In," the cake bearing your name, and all the rest. It means, clearly, that your Sisters are happy over your appointment, that they are with you. From here on, you'll have to show them that their initial confidence in you was warranted.

What's the first test you will have to pass? It's Justice. In all the books I've seen about Superiors, from Saint Bonaventure on, justice heads the lists of the virtues demanded of a Superior. A few authors, after making this demand, go into a dither about it, charging that many Superiors have not the faintest concept of justice, and by their injustice gravely harm their communities. Well, maybe a few Superiors are unjust. But many? That, it seems to me, is a question for debate.

Justice means, simply, fairness. It respects the rights of another, gives him his due. It proceeds not from charity or benignity, but plain honesty. The Ten Commandments were indited to insure it: the first three to insure divine rights, the others to insure human rights. And the courts of the world exist to enforce it.

"But," you may ask, "what rights have *religious*?" Not many, it's true; certainly not the right to go where they want and do what they want. Their vow of obedience nullified that one. But they still retain (and don't laugh) the right to life—to the food, clothing, shelter, air, recreation, and rest necessary for life. And the right to a good name—a right that they might forfeit themselves, but a right no Superior dare take from them. And the right to the full practice of religious life—with time to perform the prescribed religious exercises. And the right to a happy family life in the convent with order and peace and charity prevailing. Justice insists that the Superior endeavor to insure these rights.

There's another right of *religious* that ought to be spelled out in capital letters. I mean, the right to have confidences given to Superiors kept inviolate: personal matters discussed with the local Superior in private conferences, or with the Major Superior in canonical visitations. Once the subject has spoken, her word is dead, and the Superior becomes the grave of it forevermore. Never by any word or look or action should the Superior suggest that she has any memory of the matter.

You know how sacrosanct is the seal of Catholic confession; how a priest must give up his life, if need be, to protect that seal. Well, the confidences of a religious subject set a seal upon the lips of a Superior. Not, it's true, the seal of sacramental confession, but the seal of professional secrecy. To violate that seal is to violate justice. It is also to undermine irreparably a subject's trust in her Superior. Right on the threshold of your Superiorship, resolve that this is one injustice of which you will never never be guilty.

Next on your list of injustices to guard against, please put favoritism. Of one Superior I know, it used to be said, "That man is really impartial; he says 'No' to everybody!" Well,

better "No" to everybody than "Yes" to only a select few. To give you an example: three religious teachers went to their Superior one Friday evening many years ago, and asked permission to attend a Sigmund Romberg operetta. The Superior pursed his lips thoughtfully. "Myles," he said, "you may go, you are an organist. And, Paul, yes, you are a violinist. But, Symphorian, no, you are a tone-deaf mathematician." You'd think the three had asked for higher studies in music, for which only two of them qualified, instead of for an evening's recreation, for which all three of them qualified.

The Superior who plays favorites hurts herself, the favorites, the rest of the community. She hurts, I say, herself. She practices particular friendship, deservedly condemned by all spiritual writers. She warps her judgment by prepossessions and prejudices. She shrinks her charity till it covers not the many but only the few. She impairs her sense of spiritual values, living by feeling rather than by faith. She loses all the childlike simplicity that marks the true servant of God. For her double-dealing ways, her arbitrary rule, her manifest weakness, she forfeits the trust and respect of all her subjects, including her favorites. She is utterly unfit for office. For the good of her own soul and of the souls of her subjects, she ought to resign, performing at least that *one* act of justice towards her community.

Secondly, I repeat, the partial Superior hurts those whom she favors. She fosters their vanity by her special attention to them. She encourages their indolence by her readiness to condone it. She cuts them off from the common blessings by cutting them off from the common life. She draws their love away from God to herself. She is like an indulgent mother spoiling her children by all the surest and swiftest methods known.

During World War I, the rector of a minor seminary, an American by adoption though a German by birth, was strong

for waving Old Glory—perhaps to prove his Simon-pure patriotism. One day, at a student assembly in the study hall, he dubbed, for reasons never made quite clear, a lad named Ludwig "the Model American Boy." Ludwig, a short, dumpy, pimply boy in an expensive tweed suit, stood up and smirked, while the other boys leered. Ludwig, feeling that a model, like a king, could do no wrong or would be suspect of none, perpetrated a felony unknown in the annals of the seminary: he sneaked down the fire-escape one moonless night shortly after his canonization, went to the village store, and stuffed himself with ice cream and candy. He was caught returning. The next day Ludwig's chair in the study hall was vacant. The rector, almost in tears, announced that Ludwig had shattered his faith in Model American Boyhood. And, in the unkindly manner of youth, all the assembled students grinned with satisfaction. Here was the old, old story of the pet that became the problem. When will Superiors learn that lesson?

Thirdly, the partial Superior hurts the rest of the community. She sows among her subjects discord, envy, and uncharitableness. The non-favorites demand: "What's so special about Electa, that *she* goes on all the trips with the Superior? Why can *she* make long-distance phone-calls home whenever she wants to? How can *she* have a radio in her room?" I don't doubt that's what Jacob's sons asked some four thousand years ago about their brother Joseph, Jacob's pet: "What's so special about Joseph, that *he* should get a coat of many colors?" And I don't doubt that's what the ten Apostles asked one another when the mother of the Zebedees sought preferment for her sons: "What's so special about James and John, that in the kingdom *they* should sit closest to Christ?" (The Gospel does report that the ten were "moved with indignation against the two brethren.") Oh, there's a world of wisdom in the poet Cowper's line, "Our discontent is from comparison." In religious life we should not compare the

treatment we receive with the treatment our associates receive. We should not, but we do. So the Superior who treats all of us the same will eliminate our comparison and our discontent. His justice will keep everybody happy.

Do you want to know to what lengths Superiors can carry their favoritism? Then just recall the case of Saint Hyacintha of Mariscotti. Hyacintha, you'll remember, was no cradle saint. Far from it. Her early life was a cult of frivolity. Her only concerns were hair-do's, dresses, jewelry, dances, parties, and beaus. When a lover jilted her, she fled in shame to a convent. She entered the convent, but the convent never entered her. She had no thought of keeping any convent rule, nor, amazingly enough, did her Superior make her. She lived there rather as a fashionable boarder. Her aristocratic father richly furnished for her a cottage in the convent garden: with tapestries, draperies, rugs, hand-carved furniture. She elaborately ornamented her nun's habit with buttons and bows. She had her own servants, her own meals. And she entertained lavishly in her cottage.

Can't you imagine the unrest among the "commoners" of that community: their envy of Hyacintha's Dream House, of the spiced fragrances wafting from her kitchen, of the comings and goings of carriages, of the bright laughter and song from her parties? Hyacintha lived this lush life for ten years. Then an almost fatal illness laid her low. From her sickbed she took stock of her life and her surroundings. What she saw shocked her. Eventually she arose from that sickbed, began to do penance, and became one of the most heroic penitents of the Franciscan Order and of the Church. There is no record, however, that her Superior was ever brought to her senses by anything—that she ever amended *her* ways.

There are not, thank God, many pre-conversion Hyacinthas among us today, living the life of the world in the convent. The Council of Trent took care of such anomalies.

But are there no religious Superiors allowing unwarranted liberties to certain subjects for unwarranted reasons, purely out of favoritism? Say that two Sisters (surely, a fictitious case!) oversleep on the same morning. Will the Superior bang on the door of the one, shouting, "Do you think you are a privileged character around here?" but will she tiptoe by the door of the other, and console her after Mass, "I'm sure you're not well, Sister. Stay in, and I'll bring you your breakfast"? Or say that two Sisters have appointments with a dentist. Will the Superior mete out to the one two bus tokens, nothing more; but in addition to tokens, will she press two dollars into the hand of the other, explaining sweetly, "Just in case you need something, dear"? Her subjects know the answers to these questions.

Why does a Superior ever play favorites? One nun, whom I asked, cited three reasons: 1) A Sister, with outside contacts, can commandeer a car whenever the Superior wants one. How much better all around to get a convent car, even a second-hand one, if permissible; or to hire a cab or take a bus! We can become so intent on holy poverty that we forget it costs laymen to transport us hither and yon. Many a devout layman has lived to regret that, in a generous gesture, he once upon a time volunteered the service of his car and himself to "the good Sisters." Those good Sisters have, literally, been taking him for a ride ever since. A sound motto for religious as well as for laymen is, "Pay as you go!" 2) A Sister's dad sends the Superior a cheering check at Christmas. Good for him! But he hardly intends his check to be a Yuletide form of simony. It would be strange if the treatment accorded to each Sister by a Superior depended on the bank account of each Sisters' father; strange, indeed, for religious professing to scorn Mammon and his works and pomps. 3) A Sister is of the same nationality as the Superior. Then, on their national holiday, let them put their bonnets together and sing their national anthem—but nothing more. Certainly, God has no national preferences. He has made all men of all nations; and, as the Negro spiritual says, all His "chillun got wings." He once did have a Chosen People, the Jews. But since Good Friday afternoon, all mankind is His Chosen People. "We . . . are one body," Saint Paul insists, "in Christ" (Rom. 12:5).

After mentioning nationality as a reason for favoritism, it might not be amiss to mention race as a reason for prejudice. For religious communities do exist in which white Superiors or subjects regard non-white Sisters as religious servants. The whites may greet the non-whites with sad, little smiles; but the whites associate with them only as much as duty requires, always with the notion lurking in the whites' minds that "they're not like us," that they are second-class citizens. Obviously, blacks and reds and yellows are *not* like whites in color. So what? Does God have any preference for whites? If He favors any race, it would seem to be the non-whites, since He makes more of them (about two-thirds of all mankind, in fact). No, God is color-blind. And so, surely, must religious be. There are in heaven no downstairs pews reserved for the whites, with the blacks and the reds and the yellows consigned to the choir loft. All who go there will be, again, "all one in Christ."

To wind up our reflections on justice, recall Our Lord's parable of the vineyard workers (Matt. 20). It contains so many practical hints on justice you would think that, when Our Lord uttered it, He was looking straight at religious Superiors. First of all, the vineyard master, needing workers, went to the marketplace to hire them. That's all there was to it. He made them fill out no questionnaires, demanded no "references" from their previous employers. He simply hired them, and gave them a chance to prove themselves.

The lesson here for Superiors is clear. If a new subject comes to you, demand no dossier on her past performances.

In an unusual case (if for example, the Sister is just recovering from a nervous breakdown), it will be helpful, and perhaps even necessary, for you to know her background; and your Major Superior should inform you of it. But give the new arrival a fresh start. As a nun once remarked in this context, "Most of us do improve with age and learn from past mistakes."

Some of the vineyard workers, you remember, were called early, some were called late. It's like that in religious life. The poet-priest of the South, Father Abram Ryan, wrote, "My heart was born with priestly vestments on." Some boys' hearts are born with cords and cowls on, and some girls' hearts with nuns' veils. Others, though, find their religious vocation much later in life, as jokingly was said of one such belated arrival: "He gave his flesh to the world, and his bones to the Lord." But it is well to remember that both the early arrivals and the late have received the same call from the Master and thus merit the same treatment.

All who went into the vineyard, whether early or late, were put to work. None of them (maybe cousins or close friends of the master) were allowed to sit around in the shade and eat grapes and swap stories while the rest worked at the vines. So all in the religious community are to work, each according to the talents and the strength God has given her. The Superior should not overload "the willing horse," allowing less generous subjects to enjoy ladylike leisure, but should distribute the work in fair and equal ratio.

Finally, all the vineyard workers received the same pay, "every man a penny." Similarly, all who live the common life should share equally the temporal rewards of the common life. The Superior is not to make in those rewards the sort of distinction an old Brother cook was heard making on the telephone: "Please send a dozen fresh doughnuts for the priests, and six dozen stale doughnuts for the clerics—they like 'em stale."

Let your motto be that of the vineyard master, "Everyone shall receive a penny"—unless on occasion the convent coffers are unusually full, and you feel unusually generous, and you tell your Sisters, "Everyone shall receive a *nickel*!"

Your affectionate uncle,

FATHER C.

5. *"Be not Lifted up"*

DEAR SISTER,

You've seen, I imagine, the restored Holy Thursday rite called the *Mandatum*. In it a Father Superior kneels and washes the feet of twelve of his religious subjects, or a diocesan pastor washes the feet of twelve of his male parishioners. The rite dramatically recalls, of course, Christ's washing of the feet of the twelve Apostles during the Last Supper. And it recalls the lesson of humility Christ sought to teach them by that unusual action. After His Resurrection He would appoint them the rulers of His Church. But they were to conduct themselves not as rulers but as servants. "He that will be first among you," He charged them, "let him be your servant: even as the Son of Man is come not to be ministered unto, but to minister" (Matt. 20:27–28). Earthly rulers might rule in pomp and pride, as lords of their subjects; the Apostles were to rule in humility, as servants of their subjects.

Justifiably, then, the books on Superiorship list humility immediately after justice as a virtue demanded of a religious Superior. "Have they made thee ruler?" Solomon asks. "Be not lifted up: be among them as one of them" (Ecclus. 32:1). For "lifted up" Saint Paul says "puffed up," swollen with pride. The religious Superior is sent to a community "not to be ministered unto, but to minister"; not to receive service, but like Christ to render it.

Before reminding you what humility is, let me remind you what it is not. It is not a matter of postures, gestures, or voice. A fifth-rate actor could master this Uriah Heep kind of "humility" in two minutes. Nor is humility a matter of self-depreciation, of professing to be more sinful or more ignorant or more inept than we are: of the "I'm-a-worm-and-no-man" routine. Some of the saints could talk like that and mean what they said. But you and I cannot. The simple truth is that, though God knows we are sinful enough, we are *not* (as yet) on the F. B. I. list of the Ten Most Wanted Criminals. Whoever wrote the following lines perfectly characterized this type of humility:

Once in a fervent passion, I cried with desperate grief:
"O Lord, my soul is black with guilt. Of sinners I'm the chief!"
Then came my Guardian Angel, and whispered from behind:
"Vanity, my little man. You're nothing of the kind!"

All this moaning and groaning self-condemnation is merely a subtle effort to evoke praise from others: "You're nothing of the kind!"

There is no humility, either, in disclaiming talents we actually possess, achievements we have actually accomplished. "If," as Father Leo Trese writes, "God has been gracious enough to give us some skill, physical or mental, it would be a discourtesy to God to pretend we do not have it." A discourtesy, certainly; just as it would be a discourtesy if a benefactor had given us an air-conditioner for our chapel, to deny that we have an air-conditioner. A discourtesy—and a lie. Saint Teresa, not one to sell humility short, calls the disavowal of one's graces and gifts a downright obstacle to spiritual progress. It's the negativism of the Unprofitable Servant.

Did Mary remonstrate with the Angel Gabriel after he had hailed her as "full of grace"? ("Please, Gabriel, not *full* of grace!") Did Peter deny that at the gate of the Temple he had miraculously healed a life-long cripple? ("No, not I! It must have been the man's own power of positive thinking!") Did Paul disclaim the phenomenal number of conversions his zeal and labors had wrought? ("Statistics, you know, are often wrong!") Not in the least. But it's pertinent to note that none of these three referred their graces and accomplishments to themselves. None identified them with themselves. All of them knew their gifts *were* gifts, and referred them to God the Giver. "He that is mighty hath done great things to me," said Mary (Luke 1:49); "The author of life . . . hath given this perfect soundness," said Peter (Acts 3:15,16); "God gave the increase," said Paul (I Cor. 3:6). And that is what humility bids us do. We are to count our blessings, acknowledge them, give thanks to God for them. And when someone compliments us on an ability we have, let us, instead of protesting hypocritically, say, "Thank you"—and in our minds immediately forward the compliment to the correct address, to God Who deserves it.

All right, then, what actually is humility? As you have heard again and again in retreats, humility is truth. It's a correct estimate of oneself, Saint Thomas Aquinas explains, with a consequent contempt of oneself. It's a clear mirror that shows us exactly what we are in God's sight. And what are we? We are creatures. A certain number of years ago, fewer for you than for me, we did not exist. We were nothing, and our habitat was nowhere. Then, at a given moment in time, the Omnipotent Hand of God reached into the great void of nothingness and brought us forth into existence. And here we are today, but we are here not by our own power. The Hand of God that created us sustains us, else we should drop back in a split-second into the nothingness from which we originally came. We should be the same missing persons, the same nonentities that we were a hundred years ago. To be keenly and constantly aware of our total dependence on God ought to help us walk ever in humility. A correct self-estimate ought to insure a correct self-contempt.

Now, just as we'd be absurd if we strutted about boasting, "I am!" so we'd be absurd if we strutted about boasting,

"I am a religious!" Our religious vocation, like our existence, was not our idea or our achievement; it was God's. "You have not chosen Me," Our Lord declared, "but I have chosen you" (John 15:16). Why He chose us, only He knows. Perhaps Jeremias answers for most of us: "I have drawn thee, taking pity on thee" (Jer. 31:3).

It is truly meet and just, therefore, that we thank God daily for our religious vocation. But it is not meet and just that we look askance at those not called to the religious life, as though they were inferior souls unworthy of our high estate. This attitude, not altogether unknown among religious, smacks of the smugness of the front-pew Pharisee who wrapped his cloak about him and sighed, "I give thee thanks, O God, that I am not as the rest of men" (Luke 18:11). He, you'll recall, was *not* the one who "went down into his house justified."

But you're not only alive and a religious; you're a Superior. Does that distinction give you any cause for pride? You have the good sense to know that it doesn't. Maybe your appointment came as a medal for Distinguished Service in the ranks and maybe it didn't. Maybe it came as a prompt and unanimous decision of your Council; or maybe it came in the random, devious way an assignment of distinction came to one of my confreres some years ago. Over the phone the Provincial's Secretary told him, "Father Provincial would like you to preach the Lenten course at Saint Adam's Cathedral this year. How about it?"

"Tell Father Provincial I'd be delighted!" the friar answered promptly. He hung up the receiver. With a warm glow inside him, he mused to himself: "Well, now, out of our eight hundred priests, Father Provincial has picked little me!" The thought was tutti-fruiti gum to chew on. It cheered him through his laborious preparations for the sermons, and his preaching of them. Then on Easter Sunday he chanced to meet the Provincial. The friar beamed, "I want to thank you, Father, for that assignment!"

The Provincial looked blank. "Assignment?" he echoed.

"Yes," said the friar, wondering if Father Provincial had been working too hard lately, "that Lenten course at Saint Adam's Cathedral."

"Oh," said the Provincial, "so you're the one who gave it. I wondered. The first four men my Secretary asked all reneged."

Not meaning to belittle you, it is possible, I say, that your Superiorship came to you in that shop-worn condition. Perhaps others of less malleable spirit declined the appointment. Perhaps after long hours in session some member of your Council suggested in weary desperation: "What about Sister Clare? She might at least do no harm." Who knows what transpired in that *sanctum sanctorum?*

Another humbling reflection about your job is that it is not quite "top brass," is it? You are Superior over how many? Not over "tousands and tousands," as a proud Irish mother used to tell her neighbors about her son, the Guardian of a friary of some eighty clerics. You direct an infinitesimal percentage of the earth's teeming population. Besides, though you are up now, in a few flips of the calendar you will be down again. "Drest in a little brief authority"—Shakespeare was right.

If a Superior is "lifted up," if she lets her office go to her head, she deserves to be called Sister Truen. The truen, I've read, is an Irish bird with long, spindly legs, and with the odd habit of lying on its back with its legs up, croaking something that sounds like, "Look at me, look at me!" as if to say, "See how wonderful I am, holding up, with these two frail legs, the vast roof of the sky!" There is no need, I'm sure, to explain the parable.

Still in a narrative vein, I want to tell you about another

rare creature, a hard-headed old friar who in all of his eighty-four years never made a mistake. At least, he never admitted to having made one.

One day a young Brother found this Father standing in the friary back yard, stroking in his arms a stray cat of composite species and colors. "This," Father announced pontifically, "is a Maltese cat."

"Gosh, it looks to me," the Brother ventured, "like a common alley cat."

Father frowned at such youthful ignorance of zoology. "A Maltese cat!" he maintained. Then he added, with the finality of a Luther nailing a thesis on a church door, "Maltese cats never shed fur."

The Brother shook his head. "I don't want to contradict you, but . . . "

"Maltese cats never shed fur!" Father trumpeted, his wrath rising. He dropped the cat to the ground. Quite discernibly, his sleeves were covered with feline fur. "Except," Father added, with no less finality, "'at certain seasons!" And he strode off.

Unlike Father, you will occasionally be in the wrong. So, then, be big enough, or little enough, to admit it. Don't try to explain away a mistake by any "except at certain seasons." Everybody can see through that smoke-screen. Don't imagine that the admission of a mistake lowers the dignity of your office. It has, I'm convinced, just the opposite effect. For one thing, it shows your subjects that you are honest. For another, it ingratiates you with them. They relax and smile and say, "Thank heaven, we have a Superior who is just like us: sometimes she goofs!"

You'll not "goof" very often, however, if in matters of any moment you consult others. You have an Assistant Superior; let her assist you. You have a group of intelligent and experienced subjects; get their suggestions concerning convent and school matters. Let your faculty meetings be a free exchange of ideas, not merely a cut-and-dried announcement of your own. Make your Sisters feel that the convent and school are *theirs,* not *yours.* Saint Bonaventure cites three clear advantages that accrue to the Superior who consults others: 1) the Superior is less liable to err; 2) in case of errors, the blame will fall not exclusively on the Superior; 3) the Superior's humility will often win her unusual discernment. Even Moses, accustomed to speaking with God face to face, willingly followed the advice of his father-in-law Jethro. And even Saint Paul, though filled with the Holy Ghost, went to Jerusalem to confer with Peter and James and John, to make sure that his teaching conformed with theirs in every particular.

On my travels in retreat work, I see all types of convents, monasteries, churches, and chapels. Some are a joy to behold—attractive in their lines and furnishings, and eminently suited for their purpose. Such buildings did not just happen, like Topsy. Inquiries always reveal that they resulted from much community planning, that they incorporated every worthwhile suggestion from every member of the community. What though the plans had to be revised a dozen times? The buildings now stand with everything in them that should be there, and with no foot of space wasted. And everybody is happy over them. Other buildings, though, sadden the soul. They are shapeless, graceless, and astoundingly useless. Notwithstanding appearances, they did not just happen, either. Inquiries always reveal that they resulted from one person's planning—the Superior's. He or she consulted no one. The result? Subsequent Superiors will have to try to revamp such buildings, at the added cost of thousands, and with results still far from satisfactory. It's rather depressing, in such cases, to think of "what might have been." Why do I bring this up? Just in case you might be called on, during your tenure of office, to build anything. Please do not build even a dog-house without, first, inspecting as many dog-houses as you can without risk of life and limb; second, discussing dog-houses with your community. In that way you are not likely to end in the dog-house yourself. Nor will your successor have to rebuild your dog-house.

Another happy result of humility in a Superior is this: the Superior, aware of her own imperfections, can understand the imperfections of her subjects, and bear with their imperfections as they must bear with hers. She will not imitate the young, newly ordained priest who, in hearing his first confession, exclaimed at each fault confessed, "Inconceivable—simply inconceivable!" Rather, she will imitate a famed old confessor at Louvain who, no matter what sin a penitent confessed, used to cluck sympathetically, "Yes, yes, I've done it myself." For although the Superior may not actually have done a specific wrong that a subject has done, she knows that she is entirely capable of doing it. Every man, says Karl Stern, has in his breast a den of potential robbers and murderers. And only God's grace keeps the door of that den locked and bolted. A fearsome truth, and the humble Superior admits it.

Some Superiors, it would seem, suffer from amnesia: they completely forget their own proven peccability. As subjects they were by no means always on the side of the angels. They were known to cut many a corner. But as Superiors they become the most rigid task-masters. The least irregularity in their subjects sends them storming through corridors, shouting orders and threats and insults. There is something of the mad reformer about them, with their zeal the "bitter zeal" denounced by Saint James (James 3:11). How explain their conduct? I suppose a psychiatrist would read it as a defense mechanism. They shout to hide their insecurity. They strut on stilts to conceal their short stature. The only thing to be said in their favor is, they afford their subjects constant opportunities to merit richly by patience and charity.

Another gracious benefit of your humility will be this: it will prevent your discouragement when things go wrong.

When, I mean, your most careful plans miscarry, your hardest efforts add up to nothing, your best achievements are nullified. If in your efforts you've sought your own glory, then, indeed, will failure gall you. But if you've sought only the glory of God, then failure will not disturb the calm of your spirit. For your very efforts, though apparently sterile, have given God the glory you intended them to give. So why lose heart? Why grieve as though all is lost? Actually, nothing is lost but human applause, the loss of which is gain.

Your humility will likewise preclude all envy of your subjects. Perhaps some of them outrange you in ability, versatility, or popularity. If your pride is wounded, you may come to regard them as dangerous rivals, and try to "cut them down to size"—that is, to your size. You may subtly thwart their efforts, or undermine their reputations. Impossible, you protest? Just recall Saul's envy of David ("Saul slew his thousands," sang the women of Jerusalem beneath the palace windows, "but David slew his tens of thousands!")—and the spear that Saul hurled at David. But if you have true humility, you'll rather rejoice in the superior excellence of others. You'll act in the generous manner of Saint Bonaventure towards his good friend, Saint Thomas Aquinas. Both, you know, were appointed by Pope Urban IV to compose hymns for the upcoming new feast of Corpus Christi. Both worked hard at the assignment. But when on a visit to Saint Thomas Saint Bonaventure read the majestic hymns Thomas had composed—*Pange lingua, Adoro te devote,* and the rest—he immediately went home and tore up his own manuscripts, which, it's safe to say, were majestic enough in their own right. That's the way of the saints. Their "charity envieth not, but rejoiceth in truth."

One more boon of humility. It will enable you to leave your post gracefully when the time to leave comes. How many religious, quite ready to be told, "Friend, go up higher," are not quite so ready to hear, "Zacchaeus, descend!" To me, the remarkable thing about Saint Simon Stylites was not that he spent years atop his desert column baking in the Egyptian sun, but that at the order of his ecclesiastical Superiors he promptly slithered down. This convinced them that, unconventional as it was, his mode of life was the Will of God. Some religious, I say, are more nimble on the ascent than on the descent. They develop an at-home feeling in office, a feeling of permanent possession. When evicted from office, they act like expatriated Russian duchesses, trailing clouds of glory, constantly alluding to the grandeur of their past regime. Or like meddlesome mothers-in-law, forever telling their successors, "*I* wouldn't do it that way, Sister." Some are even permanently embittered by their deposition and, for the rest of their days, are hostile to those who deposed them and those who succeeded them. A few, in fact, angrily pull up stakes and start a community of their own, with themselves, of course, in the saddle. All of which suggests a woeful lack of religious detachment from temporalities. If you, dear Sister, do not allow yourself to become attached to your office, your removal from it will cause you no more pain than the removal of gloves from your hands. You'll say with Job: "The Lord gave and the Lord hath taken away. . . . Blessed be the name of the Lord!" (Job 1:21).

To knit the whole issue, let me remind you of Our Lord's summary description of the Pharisees: "They lord it over" their subjects. Haughty, contemptuous, cold, distant, domineering—such was the rule of these hated Jewish authorities. It goes without saying that your rule is to be the antithesis of all that. You are to "lord it over" no one in any way. You are not to flaunt your authority, perpetually pointing to your badge and insisting, "Remember, I am the Superior!" Rather, you are to de-emphasize your authority as far as it is consistent with the exercise of it. You are to be among your subjects "as one of them," regarding them as your Sisters, not as your servants. If, as the Jesuit Father John E. Moffatt puts it well, you are "solemn high" in your relations with them, you'll soon find yourself "left solemnly alone in your highness." Your subjects will approach you only when they absolutely must, and then with uneasiness. You'll be a matron in a prison rather than a mother in a home.

To be specific, don't try to "lord it over" your Sisters' private devotions—insisting that, because you feel tenderly towards the Fourteen Holy Helpers, so must your subjects. Hear Saint Francis de Sales on this point: "Generous devotion does not wish to have companions in all that it does, but only in its aim, which is the glory of God and the advancement of our neighbor in divine love; and provided it sees the neighbor so advancing, it cares little what road is taken to reach the goal." And don't try to "lord it over" the common menu—like a Superior who doted on sauerkraut, and so had it served daily to his community. And don't try to "lord it over" the little free time your subjects have—as did a Superior who, with a passion for activity that out-Marthaed Martha, routed her subjects from a rare holiday siesta exclaiming: "Be up and doing! Time is God's gift!" Rest, you know, is also God's gift. And don't try to "lord it over" the recreation period —turning it because you're a lover of song into a "Sing-along-with-Sister-Superior" command performance. Finally, don't try to "lord it over" the general conversation—like the Autocrat of the Breakfast Table or like Shakespeare's Sir Oracle: "When I ope my lips, let no dog bark." Let your role be that of the interlocutor in the oldtime minstrel show—not dominating the talk, but stimulating it.

Don't, in a word, try to remake your subjects according to your own image and likeness, no matter how perfect you may be persuaded it is!

Your affectionate uncle,

FATHER C.

6. *"Have Confidence in the Lord"*

Dear Sister,

If ever a man was reluctant to don authority, surely, that man was Moses. Recall how, when Moses was shepherding Jethro's flock one day on Mount Horeb, God spoke to him from the midst of a flaming bush.

God clearly identified Himself: "I am the God of Abraham, of Isaac, of Jacob. I am who am."

And Moses clearly recognized the Speaker as God: he "hid his face, for he durst not look at God."

God then announced that He had chosen Moses as His ambassador to plead with Pharao to let the Israelites leave Egypt.

Moses demurred: "Who am I that I should go to Pharao and should bring forth the children of Israel out of Egypt?"

God assured him: "I will be with thee."

Moses objected: "They will not believe me."

God answered by giving him, then and there, miraculous powers as his credentials.

Moses tried another loop-hole: "I am not eloquent. I have slowness of tongue."

God countered: "Who hath made man's mouth? I will be in thy mouth: I will teach thee."

Cornered, Moses simply pleaded: "I beseech thee, Lord, send whom thou wilt send"—meaning, "Send anybody, but not *me!*" At this point in the debate, the Lord, understandably enough, grew "angry" with Moses—with Moses' stubborn opposition to His express Will.

Moses had admirable humility. He really knew himself

and contemned himself. No question about that. But he lacked a virtue meant to supplement humility, to prevent humility from becoming static and sterile. He lacked confidence in God and in himself as God's choice. He was right in realizing, "I am nothing"; but he was wrong in not realizing, "God is everything." And, as you know, his lack of confidence in God ultimately barred his entrance into the Promised Land, towards which he had led his people for forty difficult years.

Well, it's of this virtue of confidence I would remind you today. It's a beauteous virtue, calm and clear and as full of stars as a mountain lake on a cloudless summer night. It's an invigorating virtue, full of April sunlight that gently and silently persuades all the land to bud and blossom. It's the tranquil atmosphere in which Superior and subjects alike live happiest and work best. And it's generated by a Superior's confidence in God, herself, and her subjects.

Why should you as Superior have even a mite of confidence in yourself? Because, although neither a saint nor a genius (Moses wasn't, either), you are God's choice as Moses was. God put you into office. Of yourself, you are incapable of any worthwhile achievement; but God is capable. He will use you as His instrument, if you allow Him. So, as Solomon urges, "have confidence in the Lord with all thy heart, and lean not on thy own prudence. In all thy ways, think on him, and he will direct thy steps" (Prov. 3:5,6). Perhaps you have read how, in the early days of his reign, Pope John XXIII was much troubled by the loneliness of his august authority. His sleep was frequently disturbed by dreams from which he would awake saying, "I must take that up with the Pope." Then, as his mind cleared, he would say to himself, "But *I* am the Pope!" With a sigh he would sink back on his pillow saying, "I must take that up with the Lord." His remarkable reign was proof that, truly, the Lord directed his steps.

As Superior, you *must* make decisions, you *must* act. In

all important matters, you will of course pray, and deliberate, and consult others who may well be God's messengers. Then, I say, you must act. That's something that Saint Angela Merici could not bring herself to do regarding the founding of her Ursuline Order. Christ had told her, in repeated visions, to found that Order. But she hesitated, always, of course, leaning on her own prudence. At length Christ ordered her bluntly, "Go, do My Will!" And she did and her Order prospered mightily right from its start.

I don't mean to imply that all your undertakings will be so clearly heaven-directed or so richly heaven-blest. Some will fizzle like Roman candles shot into rain. Some won't even ignite. You simply cannot avoid making some mistakes. But certainly you will make fewer mistakes by action than by inaction. Babe Ruth, you know, was called the King of Swat. That doesn't mean that the Babe walloped a home run every time he went to bat. In fact, he frequently struck out. It means that, first, he batted whenever he was supposed to,; and, second, he hit more home runs than any of the other players, though his batting average hovered annually around .300, not around 1.000. Well, in the same way, you must act whenever called to action. Not all your actions will be smashing successes. Frequently you will fail altogether. Your general average will establish you as a successful—or unsuccessful—Superior. But, remember, you'll have no average at all unless you act, act, act.

Listen to this golden advice from Saint Francis de Sales: "Undertake all your affairs with a calm and peaceful mind, and endeavor to dispatch them in order, one after another. In all your affairs, rely wholly on God's Providence, through which alone we must look for success. Nevertheless, labor quietly on your part to cooperate with its designs." Notice his words: "calm . . . peaceful . . . order . . . quietly." He wants you to work without worry; for worry distracts you from doing well the very work about which you worry. He wants you to work without haste; for haste ever makes waste. He wants you to work in orderly fashion, performing cleanly and efficiently one task at a time; for order is heaven's first law. He wants you, as the saying goes, to work as though everything depended on you, and to trust as though everything depended on God. And he wants you to place the finished product in God's Hands and leave it there. To work in that way is to work with confidence.

The opposite side of the coin is diffidence, no more a virtue in a Superior than in a traffic cop. Picture for a moment Officer Diffident. There he stands, police whistle in hand, at a busy intersection of streets. Traffic is converging on him from four directions. Pedestrians are accumulating on the sidewalks like ice-jams. He glances nervously before and aft, right and left. He toys with his whistle. Cars and buses and trucks begin to honk their horns. Pedestrians begin to shout for action. Still he just can't make up his mind. He shuts his eyes tight, and with nods and crotchety gestures tries to outline his plans. Finally, as the clamor and din reach deafening volume, he quits his post and heads for black coffee in a nearby diner. I don't expect he will be cited for excellence in the fulfillment of duty, do you?

Has a diffident religious Superior nothing in common with this cartoon cop? Look at her desk. It's a jumble of letters and bills and receipts and pads and pencils and books and reports. Look at her bulletin-board. It's cluttered with obsolete lists and notices, full of pencilled-in changes; it's singularly devoid of lists and notices of current significance. She will pass the word around, if she remembers. Look at her rule of her subjects. She somehow can't make up her mind to say "Yes" or "No," "Come" or "Go." The result is confusion compounded, a snarl in traffic that drives all in it to desperation. Such a

Superior, it seems to me, ought to retire for black coffee—permanently, that is.

Some Superiors, though able to reach decisions, make a cult of worrying. They worry if a Sister gets a telegram or a long-distance phone call ("Did her father drop dead?"); if a Sister is five minutes overdue returning from a trip to the oculist's ("Did she step in front of a truck?"); if a Sister has an appendectomy ("Is it peritonitis, Doctor?"); if a Sister is long in the confessional ("Is she discussing a dispensation from her vows?"); if a Sister is changed to another convent ("How will we ever get along without her?"); if a Sister is popular with her pupils ("Is she too easy with them?"); if a Sister is unpopular with her pupils ("Is she too strict?"); if the pastor never visits the convent ("Have we offended him in some way?"); if the pastor visits the convent regularly ("Is he checking on us for the bishop?"). They even worry if they have nothing to worry about ("Things have been going *too* well around here lately!"). And their worries frequently create problems that otherwise would not have existed.

A typical phenomenon of this sort occurred in the Canadian Province of Saskatchewan in July, 1962. Nine hundred physicians in that province, you may recall, went on a strike at that time against their government's newly launched program of socialized medicine. Well, immediately a rash of heart-attacks occurred there—caused by what? Caused by people's worrying what they'd do if they suffered heart-attacks in those doctorless days. A popular song used to promise that "wishing can make it so." Wishing, of course, can make nothing so, or most of the populace would be millionaires. But it is a medical fact that worrying can make it so, can induce quite a few physical disorders about which the worriers worry.

The Bureau of Standards in Washington, D. C., conducted experiments with fog some years ago. They discovered that a dense fog covering seven city blocks is actually composed of less than a glass of water. Yet this fog envelops in gray gloom seven city blocks, impedes vision, slows traffic almost to a standstill. Worry, even a little of it, acts like that. It shrouds one's thoughts in melancholy, quenches the vision of God's Providence, hinders movement and work. "Have confidence in the Lord with all thy heart." That confidence ought to be the bright sun that dissipates any gathering fog. As a Superior—I say it again—you do God's work; can you not expect God's help? Do your best, and trust in Him. If you make worry your cup and portion, you invite ulcers. It's said that ulcers are a common complaint on Wall Street, among men who anxiously follow the daily fluctuations of the Dow-Jones averages. But ulcers, as symptomatic at least of worry, ought to be unknown among religious, whose fortunes are in the Hands of the Christ who never changes, who is "the same yesterday, today, and forever."

Along with confidence in God and in yourself as His appointed agent, you need abundant confidence in your subjects. Trust in them, first, because they are religious. If they were prison inmates, you might suspect them of constantly plotting new felonies. But they are God's elite, each chosen by Him out of tens of thousands, each the object of His special love. Now, I think I know nuns (as far as any mere male can know any women). I was taught by them in grammar school. I had, as you well know, a sister and five cousins in the convent. As a priest I have given conferences and retreats to hundreds of nuns, and have heard the confessions of thousands. And from all my contacts with nuns I hail them sincerely as the noblest human beings that walk this earth. They are the glory of the Church, her Exhibit-A in her claims to holiness. Being human, they have, of course, human faults. But underneath those faults they are amazingly earnest, willing, devout, self-sacrificing, God-fearing, God-loving, God-serving women. I tip my capuche to them all!

Surely, such people merit supreme trust. They need no house-detective to check their motives and actions; their own consciences do the checking. A Superior, yes, but not a house-detective. Distrust, therefore, any derogatory reports about any of them; insist on first hearing the reported Sister's side of the story. Put the most favorable interpretation possible on their words and actions and you will rarely err. Accept the general thesis that, like you, all of them are trying to know, love, and serve God, though, like you, not always succeeding perfectly in their efforts; that, like you, all of them hope ultimately to be happy with God forever in heaven.

And, in addition to trusting in them as religious, trust in them as adults. It's hard, you know, for parents to realize that their children grow up, but their children do. And it's equally hard at times for Superiors to realize that Sisters whom they knew as giggly novices are now mature adults, but they are. They deserve, consequently, to be treated as adults. Given assignments, they should be allowed to fulfill them without the Superior's nervous supervision and interference. A baby, as Bishop Francis C. Kelley points out, would never learn to walk if mamma always carried it or wheeled it around in a gocart. Mamma must see to it, of course, that the baby doesn't walk too soon, else it will become bow-legged, like an infantile rodeo rider. But mamma cannot walk for the baby. That the baby must do for itself, and plump on its little rear now and then in the process. In exactly this same way must a religious learn to walk by walking: by getting assignments with some responsibility attached to them, and by fulfilling them on her own. She will blunder a bit, but she will learn.

One of the snappy sayings popular in the days of my youth used to be, "Let George do it." Who George was, nobody knew, except that he was the other fellow. Nowadays that phrase has turned into, "Do it yourself!" The idea, of course, carries a strong appeal to male avarice ("You can do it six times cheaper yourself!") or to male vanity ("You *can* do it yourself!"). So millions are doing it themselves in their spare time are tiling bathroom walls, cutting children's hair, soundproofing rumpus rooms, cultivating azaleas, building outdoor grills, painting pictures, laying concrete walks, moulding ceramic what-nots, and on and on. You name it, they're doing it themselves. But most of them sadly discover that, despite all their do-it-yourself tool kits and libraries, they can't do everything themselves. The bank teller finds his thumb more adept with greenbacks than with lettuce. The high school teacher finds he can hammer home dates better than nails. The haberdasher finds he can fit hats on heads more easily than stones on walls. Most of them find that, in pursuing the do-it-yourself phantom, they have spent themselves, their time, and their money in vain. And in the end they look up the yellow pages of the phone book and dial for professionals to come and do it for them.

You know the point I'm getting at: don't be a do-it-yourself Superior. Don't, for instance, do all the convent book-keeping yourself, instead of getting help from some of your mathematics teachers. Don't draw up the menus and order the food yourself, instead of letting your cook exercise these liberties. Don't buy and arrange the altar flowers yourself, instead of leaving these matters to your sacristan. Don't select the new books for the library yourself, instead of giving your librarian leeway to do so. Don't chauffeur the convent car on all trips yourself, instead of letting Sisters drive who owned cars before they entered the convent. Don't spoon out medicine to a sick Sister yourself, instead of letting your infirmarian take care of her. "You must lovingly leave some work to others," advises Saint Francis de Sales, "and not seek to have all the crowns.

The ardor of holy love, which urges you to want to do everything, ought also to keep you back and make you leave others something to do for their consolation." Yes, for their consolation, and also for the better performance of the work.

I'm thinking, in this context, of a pastor I used to know. I would dub him unqualifiedly the most zealous pastor I have ever met. In fact, he was over-zealous. He did everything in the parish: instructed all the converts, answered all the sick-calls, performed all the baptisms and weddings and funerals, preached all the sermons, administered all the temporalities. And in the meantime off in corners sat his two able, young assistants, yawning and twirling their thumbs, all their youthful zeal going to rust. Yes, they were allowed to catechize children twice a week, to count the Sunday collections, and to call out numbers at Bingo. But that was all.

It's a pity, I think, that this pastor forgot the story of Jethro and Moses (Exod. 18:13–26). Jethro, Moses' father-in-law, watched Moses holding court among the Israelites in the desert from dawn till dark, settling all their petty squabbles. Jethro said to Moses: "Why sittest thou alone? Thou art spent with foolish labor: the business is above thy strength, thou alone canst not bear it." Jethro then urged Moses to restrict himself to those things that pertained directly to God—to explaining to the people the Law of God, and directing them in the worship of God. "And provide out of all the people," he continued, "able men, such as fear God, in whom there is truth, and that hate avarice, and appoint of them rulers of thousands, and of hundreds, and of fifties, and of tens; who may judge the people at all times. And when any great matter soever shall fall out, let them refer it to thee: that so it may be lighter for thee, the burden being shared out unto others." And Moses had the good sense to do as Jethro had advised him.

To free Himself for the work of His mission among men,

Our Lord turned over to Judas the finances of the Apostolic group. And He let Judas remain treasurer even after Judas had begun to abuse his office. To free themselves for the "ministry of the word," the Apostles delegated to deacons the table-serving (which had absorbed the time and energy of the Apostles themselves) in the early Christian community at Jerusalem. Why should any religious Superior today hesitate to follow such worthy precedents?

Trust in God, trust in yourself as His appointee, trust in your subjects. Do this, and "the flowers that bloom in the spring" will bloom all the year around in the little world of Sister Clare.

Your affectionate uncle,

FATHER C.

7. *"An Understanding Heart"*

Dear Sister,

In his book of essays, *Wheat and Chaff* (which I think is all wheat), Father Francis P. Donnelly, S. J., tells of a czar of Old Russia who wanted a railroad built and went about it in typical czarish fashion. He summoned his engineers, spread out before them a map of his vast country, pointed to two widely separated cities with ranges of mountains between them, drew a straight line with a ruler from the one city to the other, and said, "There! Build the railroad on that line!" Well, if you were a czar (or czarina), you could similarly draw a straight line and tell your subjects, "There! Follow that line!" But you would find that it's easier to dynamite your way through mountains than through human minds and wills. You would find that, as Father Donnelly says, when you deal with human beings, the straight line is not always the shortest distance between two points. The shortest distance is often the curved line, the circuitous line. The round-about route is not the route of cowardice; it is the route of prudence.

And what is prudence? Webster defines it well: "The ability to regulate and discipline oneself through the exercise of reason; the provident use of resources." Prudence is ordinarily equated with "good sense." It acts as an airplane navigator to a pilot: tells what can or cannot be done, what should or should not be attempted. Prudence is listed, as your third-graders in school know, as the first of the Cardinal Virtues, but it is really the guardian angel of all the virtues. Prudence keeps piety from degenerating into pietism; charity, into humanitarianism; chastity, into prudery; obedience, into servility; humility, into spinelessness; zeal, into fanaticism. Prudence was the one gift that, offered a choice of whatever he wanted, Solomon asked of the Lord: "Give to thy servant an understanding heart, to judge thy people and discern between good and evil" (III Kings 3:9).

The prudent Superior, entering on office, takes for her motto: "I will change nothing—at least for a year." She presumes the procedures established by her predecessors were established to suit the needs of the convent. So she follows them. It's possible that, with the passing of the months, she may wonder about some of those procedures, may see ways to better them. But she will "make haste slowly." She will weigh carefully the pro's and con's of any changes she contemplates and will discuss them with "the old guard." Her prayer will be one that a certain prudent Superior had on a placard on his desk: "God grant me the serenity to accept the things I cannot change, the courage to change the things I can, and the wisdom to know the difference."

The imprudent Superior seems to take for her motto: "Behold, I make all things new." She at once detects the mistakes of her predecessors, and at once sets about righting them. She installs or removes doors. She plants or pulls up shrubbery. She clears the house of the old statues ("The abomination of desolation," she calls them). She revises the *horarium.* She is the new broom that sweeps clean, and cares not how much irritant dust it raises. Her overweening self-confidence stems, of course, from her overweening conceit.

The prudent Superior rules her community with a restrained use of authority. She follows the same recipe in governing as in soft-boiling an egg: "Don't overdo it!" She gives few orders, and always quietly. Her authority acts like yeast, silently leavening the dough—not like TNT, scattering it. She doesn't ask her subjects to do inane things, in the medieval manner of planting cabbages upside down. She knows that even the sensible command is difficult enough for subjects to carry out.

The prudent Superior tries to appoint the right subject to the right task. This statement recalls an incident that occurred one evening in a clericate somewhere. The clerics had assembled in the choir loft of the parish church adjoining their monastery, to sing at Benediction. But the class organist was absent—abed with a cold.

The Superior scanned the group. "Josephus," he said, pointing to one of the clerics, "play the organ."

Josephus protested, "But, Father, I don't know how to play the organ."

"You play the violin, don't you?" pursued the Superior.

"Yes, but the violin's no keyboard instrument."

"Now, don't be difficult," the Superior insisted; "play the organ."

Josephus again pleaded his ignorance.

"All right, then," concluded the Superior, "I command you: Josephus, play the organ!"

Shaking his head incredulously, Josephus sat down at the console and pressed organ keys. It is said that in the long history of church music no sounds have ever emanated from organ pipes like those Josephus produced that evening.

Now, if I were advising Josephus, I should say: "You did what you were told to do. By human standards, the result was noise; by divine standards, the result was glorious music." But if I were advising that Superior, I should ask: "Why did you act so obtusely, making a travesty of obedience? It's true, subjects aren't supposed to reason why; but you are. Why pick a name out of a capuche when making assignments, instead of picking subjects fitted for them by nature, grace, and training? Why fatuously try to force square pegs into round holes, when you have round pegs if you look for them?"

Remember, "the provident use of resources" is part of the definition of prudence.

The imprudent Superior moves in a whirlwind. As a subject she was not particularly notable for religious observance; as a Superior she is intolerant of the least irregularity. An imprudent Superior gives utterly impossible orders, and brooks no explanations when those orders go unfulfilled. Her motto is: "I will it; I command it; my will is my reason." A biography of an ex-nun (so boringly clinical I won't even name it) tells of this sort of irrational Superior who demanded to know what book a Sister's spiritual director had given her to read. (To save you suspense, it was a classic by Saint Teresa of Avila.)

Sister replied, "I consider this a conscience matter."

The Superior repeated her demand.

Sister countered, "I'll return the book unread rather than tell you its title."

"Either way," persisted the Superior, "I must know. Or else I'll report you to Mother Provincial!"

"And I'll report you," countered Sister, "to my spiritual director!"

So went the Saga of the Unnamed Book. It's this kind of Superior whose nagging drives subjects out of their minds or out of their convents.

A prudent Superior consults others, not deeming herself Solomon, Plato, Aristotle, Augustine, and Aquinas all rolled into one. She heeds the injunction: "Do thou nothing without counsel, and thou shalt not repent when thou hast done" (Ecclus. 32:24). Hence she makes no colossal blunders under which subsequent generations of her Sisters must groan: in building, in opening new houses or closing old ones, in making drastic changes in policy. In addition to learning from others, she delights her subjects by making them feel that they count. The imprudent Superior consults nobody. She is persuaded that she knows all the answers, when, in fact, she doesn't even know all the questions. The result of her self-opinionatedness is a community of jangled nerves, dissatisfaction, strife.

The prudent Superior knows how to administer the goods of the community. Sisters have, tribally, the laudable instincts of the Valiant Woman of the Book of Proverbs: the woman who brought "her bread from afar" (Sisters go to the supermarket where it's a cent cheaper); who "considered a field and bought it" (Sisters spot the property they want, bury medals in it, get it for a song—or a psalm); who "looked well to the paths of her house" (Sisters are the world's best housekeepers). With womanly genius for detail, they know how to select, bargain, conserve. Men, tribally, lack the patience for details. On a hunch, a male Superior spends $300 on a miraculous lawn fertilizer that kills the sickly grass, or buys vats of bargain floor-wax that eats holes in the linoleum, or slaps up a building that's no sooner finished than it needs costly renovations, or lets property deteriorate till the repairing of it amounts to the rebuilding of it. I sometimes think there ought to be a special community of nuns—perhaps the Sisters of Martha—to handle the temporalities of us hapless male religious. In all mundane transactions they would see that we got our money's worth.

The prudent Superior shows herself ever willing to help her subjects in spiritual matters if they seek her help. Yet she knows that Canon Law forbids her to demand of any of them a manifestation of conscience. Her prudence will dictate that certain spiritual problems of her subjects can best be dealt with by the confessor. He is the spiritual physician, she is not. The imprudent Superior tries to X-ray her subjects' souls, consciences, and to prescribe for all ailments of the spirit.

And, finally, the prudent Superior knows when not to act—when action would be futile. It's useless and unhealthy to butt your head against a concrete wall—or against a subject immovable in her ways. It's unwise, unless you are a track champion, to poke at a hornets' nest. It's alleged that, if you come upon a bear in a woods, the best strategy is to play dead, in perfect silence and immobility. Whether this strategy really works or not, I can't testify. But I do know that it's often the only strategy to invoke towards human bears: keep quiet and do nothing.

Well, dear Sister, here is another requisite of Superiors, the "understanding heart," the saving virtue of prudence. So let your constant and fervent prayer, and the preface to all your actions, be, *Virgo prudentissima, ora pro me!*

Your affectionate uncle,

FATHER C.

8. *"Charity is Patient"*

DEAR SISTER,

En route to Jerusalem with His Apostles one day, Our Lord wanted to take a short-cut through Samaria. He sent James and John, those Sons of Thunder, ahead to a town in that territory to arrange overnight lodgings for the group. The Samaritans, you know, cordially despised the Jews; and every door in the town that opened to the knocking of James and John promptly slammed shut in their faces. In high dudgeon the two returned to Christ and asked Him: "Lord, wilt thou that we command fire to come down from heaven and consume them?" Our Lord rebuked them, saying: "You know not of what spirit you are," that is, "Your spirit is not My spirit; for I am meek of heart." And He added in explanation: "The Son of Man came not to destroy souls, but to save" (Luke 8:54–56).

Isaias says with beautiful simplicity, "The Lord waiteth" (Isa. 30:18). And why does He wait? "He dealeth patiently for your sake," Saint Peter answers, "not willing that any should perish" (II Peter 3:9). Men may ignore Him, spurn His claims, deny His very existence; yet He waits. His patience is His love waiting at the gate for the Prodigal Son to come back home.

Haste was simply not one of Our Lord's characteristics. He waited some four thousand years after the fall of Adam before He came into this world. He waited thirty of His thirty-three years before He began His public mission among men. Though the greatest Teacher of all time, he waited patiently for results in His Apostles. Surely, they were slow pupils; yet He never upbraided them or ridiculed them for their slowness. And how patiently He dealt with their faults! He reproved Peter, who had disclaimed any acquaintance with Him, merely with a glance (Luke 22:61). He called Judas, who had sold Him for thirty pieces of silver, "Friend" (Matt. 26:50). He rebuked Thomas, who had stubbornly doubted His resurrection, only with the gentle comment: "Blessed are they who have not seen, and have believed" (John 20:29).

His patience, dear Sister, must be yours. You must try to maintain something of His calm, His equanimity. You must wait for results as He waited. You must keep your head even when, as Kipling says, "all about you are losing theirs and blaming it on you." Otherwise you will be a nervous wreck before the first snow flies.

This letter would run on too long if I went into the need of patience with your own shortcomings and mistakes. I'll dispatch this topic with a story about a new home-owner who sowed grass around his new house. The grass came up, all right, but with it came a crop of dandelions. The man pulled them out by the roots. A week later he found another crop of dandelions, bright and yellow, smiling up at him. He pulled those out. When a third crop appeared, he wrote to the Bureau of Agriculture in Washington for pamphlets on the scientific extermination of dandelions. He followed all the directions meticulously—yet the dandelions kept coming. Finally on a hot Saturday afternoon in July, as he sat sweat-soaked on his porch step after another vain bout with dandelions, this thought came to him: "Look, it's evident I'll never get rid of dandelions, so I might as well learn to *love* dandelions." He did so and lived happily ever afterwards.

Now, your faults are dandelions. They're weeds; and you may not, of course, learn to love them, to live contentedly with them. Yet in your striving to eradicate them you should remember two truths: 1) Some faults you'll ever have. Human nature cannot achieve full perfection this side of the grave. 2) God demands that you try, not that you succeed. A saint, someone has well said, is a sinner who keeps on trying. So, as God is patient with you, try to be patient with yourself.

Then there's your Superiorship. What a fund of patience you need with its labors and duties and harassments! As Our Lord fed the souls of men with truth and their bodies with bread, you must cater to the spiritual and temporal needs of your subjects. You must be "all things to all men"; now giving a lifting word to a downcast subject (when you could use, so much, a lifting word yourself); now giving a willing ear to one subject's childish complaints against another (when you could validly complain, if you wanted to, against both of them); now correcting, because you must, the blatant faults of subjects (when so acutely aware of your own); now phoning to inquire discreetly why the convent confessor hasn't come for three weeks (when you really wish he would stay away permanently and someone else would be appointed), or why the chaplain hasn't appeared at 7:00 for the 6:30 convent Mass (when you know he will go into a huff over your call); now summoning a plumber to open choked drains, or a roofer to mend leaking spouts, or a carpenter to make fast a wobbly banister, or a repairman to see why the washer won't wash, or a garage man to see what's gone wrong under the hood of the convent car—not to mention calls by salesmen and itinerant beggars and parents of school children in trouble. Saint Paul says, "Everyone must bear his own burden." But you, in addition to your own, must bear the burdens of all your subjects. And I surmise that daily you find "sufficient for the day is the burden thereof."

On some days you may even be tempted to do what a desperate bus driver once did in Washington, D. C. It was one of the summer's sultriest, stickiest days; all the passengers in this driver's bus seemed either mad with the heat or corporately possessed by the devil. They refused to budge when the driver asked them to move to the rear. A drunkard, insisting it's a free country, challenged him to a fight. Two babies kept screaming at the tops of their lungs. Three women, engrossed in gossip, rode past their stop, then shrilly blamed the driver. Four teen-agers tried to slip him outdated transfers, then, forced to surrender coins, sought redress by buzzing constantly for stops. An old man opened a window; an old woman, behind him, complained at once of drafts. And so it went, until the driver's patience ran out. Giving them all a baleful glare in his mirror, he pulled to a curb, stopped, alighted from the bus saying, "Youse can all drop dead!"—and walked off the scene.

You'll have black days like that. Especially, I'd say, in March. That month seems to be the very nadir of the year. It's the month when, after the long, gray winter and the confinement it imposes, teachers are jumpiest, pupils are oneriest and skirmishes are the order of the day. On many a March day you will feel like stopping the bus, consigning the whole cantankerous crowd of passengers to perdition, and walking off. But, unfortunately, you'll have to stay at the wheel. "Beware the ides of March!" You'd better make a novena to Saint Patrick and Saint Joseph for patience to carry on till April, when windows open and tensions relax.

In addition to patience with yourself and your office, you need a Job's patience with your subjects. Monsignor Knox observes that, since suffering is good for us, God wants us to suffer: to suffer not only from heat and cold and hunger and fatigue and sickness and other natural causes beyond our control; but to suffer also from our associates—from their faults, idiosyncrasies, blunders. And suffer we do. Almost any contact with others challenges our patience in one way or another.

The basic reason is, of course, that others differ from us (a matter for later consideration).

The all-perfect religious community has never yet existed, and it never will exist. There were rebels even among the angels; even among the Apostles there were braggarts, self-seekers, cowards, and one traitor. Please don't expect, then, that *your* community will be a Communion of Saints. And please don't lose patience with it because it isn't that. Alter the following lines a bit by putting "community" for "world" and "indifferent" for "bad" and you have a safe maxim to guide you:

> Take the world as you find it. There are good and
> bad in it,
> And good and bad will be from now till the end.
> And those that expect to make saints in a minute
> Are in danger of marring more souls than they mend.

You must often settle for the second best. It isn't a question of what orders you're entitled to give, but what orders your subjects are likely to follow. If you are content to lead them rather than prod them, they will generally follow you with a will.

I once knew an old German choirmaster who had a highly combustible temper. If anyone sang a wrong note in a rehearsal, he would shout, "Dumkopf!" ("Blockhead!"), and would break his baton and tear up his music. On one occasion he hurled his spectacles to the floor and smashed them; on another, his watch. You would think his choristers sang wrong notes with malice aforethought, instead of out of amateur ignorance. How much more sensible if, instead of exploding, that director had said quietly: "No, that's not it. Listen now to the right note. Now sing it, please." To draw a parallel: when your subjects do wrong, they seldom if ever act out of malevolence or defiance of your authority, but out of human ignorance or human frailty. The way to correct them, then, is not by inveighing wildly against them, but by gently reminding them of what's right. "For the anger of man worketh not the justice of God" (Jas. 1:20).

Of the impatient Superior, Father John E. Moffat, S. J., writes these strong words: "God help the community ruled over by an impatient, grumpy, crotchety Superior! Her constant irritability or her frequent explosive outbursts keep the community in a ferment of fearful expectancy of the sudden storms that are always brewing." I once heard a Sister conducting class, as I was saying Mass in the basement church directly below Sister's classroom. From *Introibo* to *Ite missa est* Sister screamed: "I said, shut up! . . . Sit up straight! . . . Stupid, that's *not* the answer! . . . You there, turn around! . . . Bring that note to me! . . . Who threw that chalk? . . . Take that gum out of your mouth! . . . What are you drawing? . . . Stop that sniffling!"—et cetera, et cetera, all of her utterances in italics and followed by quivering exclamation points. I kept envisioning her pupils, a squirming, twitching roomful of young neurotics. (I think her name was or ought to have been—Sister Thunderhead.)

Maybe the impatient Superior suffers from high blood-pressure. If so, she is as unfit for office as a one-armed man is for violin-playing. Her anger distorts her judgment, as lightning disturbs a TV picture, filling the screen with jagged, jumping lines. It renders her incapable of dealing sanely with her subjects. She magnifies trifles. She not infrequently strikes the innocent with her bolts. She is a tornado leaving nought in its wake but ruin and human misery. She is the horrible antithesis of everything that a religious Superior ought to be: not a mother, but a monster; not a loving shepherd of her flock, but a ravening wolf that tears it to pieces. God help, indeed, her subjects!

On a car radio, I happened to tune in one afternoon to a program in which a psychiatrist was solving the problems of perturbed housewives. He was reading aloud a letter from a woman who signed herself "Vexed" and whose problem was that her husband habitually splashed water on the bathroom floor and dropped ashes on the living room carpet. What, she asked, should she do? The obvious answer seemed to be: "Get the mop and the carpet-sweeper." But, no. The psychiatrist, in his best baritone, sympathized with Vexed, then gave her this prescription: "Go into a tantrum with your husband. Blow off steam. Repression can harm you." I wondered about that advice. I wondered, if Vexed blew off steam at 5:30 p.m., what would prevent her from having a new surcharge of steam at 6:30, and 7:30, and 8:30? Vexed should, I'm sure, rather have been told to get rid of her steam-generator: to learn to control her temper through patience with her insouciant spouse. She should have been told that charity, which begins at home, "is patient."

You, dear Sister, in many unwitting ways tax the patience of your subjects—maybe by your grave manner today and your excessively cheerful manner tomorrow; maybe by a dozen of your mannerisms of speech and conduct. Well, then, isn't it only fair exchange that your subjects tax *your* patience now and then?

Your affectionate uncle,

FATHER C.

9. "I *Know Mine*"

Dear Sister,

One hot Saturday afternoon in August, one of our friar priests, the pastor of a small parish in Virginia, was busy cleaning his church. Barefoot, in dirty shirt and overalls, he was mopping the center aisle when the church door slowly opened and an ancient, wizened Negro peered in. The Negro stared at Father for a moment, then quietly closed the door. Father hurried to the door as the old man was hobbling down the steps. "Come in, Dad," he called. "Want to see the church?"

The old man hesitated, and softly asked, "Is you, suh, de bishop?"

"No," said Father, "I'm just the pastor."

With a knowing smile and a wag of his finger, the old Negro replied: "Y'all can't fool me. Ah knows a bishop when Ah sees one!"

Now, I know a real Sister Superior when I see one. By what do I know her? By her air of authority? her managerial ability? her business acumen? her effective leadership? Not at all. I know her by her motherliness. Her subjects may not call her "Mother" (a pity, say I, that the title has been dropped by so many Sisterhoods, including yours), but a mother to them she is, with a mother's tender love for each of them, a mother's concern for their welfare, a mother's interest in their efforts and pride in their achievements, a mother's joy in their joys and sorrow in their sorrows. "God is love," says Saint John. A mother, too, is love. So, as Thackeray wrote, "Mother is the name for God in the lips and hearts of little children." And "Mother" should be the name for God in the lives of a Sister Superior's subjects.

The Mother General of a mid-western Sisterhood once conducted me on an inspection tour through their new Motherhouse. There were nuns, novices, and postulants everywhere. What impressed me indelibly was not the splendid building, but the light that came into every face, like a sudden sunrise, at Mother's approach, and the personal word she dropped to everyone we met.

"Father, this is Sister Anna," she said. "Sister is ninety—but see what lovely needlework she still does!" Sister Anna, in her wheelchair, chuckled happily . . . "Father, this is Sister Cecilia, our choir-directress. And does she fill our chapel with heavenly music!" Sister Cecilia smiled demurely . . . "Father, these two novices, Sister Louise and Sister Antoinette, bake all our bread—and it's the original Wonder Bread!" The two novices giggled ecstatically. "Father, this little postulant is Mary Ann Smith, from Los Angeles. She is a trained nurse, and are we happy to have her with us!" Mary Ann blushed beatifically. And so it went: a question to this one about her sinus trouble; a comment to that one on her attractive arrangement of altar flowers; a word of encouragement to a third working on a thesis in the library; a word of praise to a fourth on the mirror-like gleam of the corridor she had just finished buffing. Throughout that tour, I seemed to hear the words of the Good Shepherd: "I know mine, and mine know Me" (John 10:14). Mother most certainly knew hers, loved hers, and took unfeigned motherly interest in their welfare, work, problems, needs. And they in return knew her and loved her.

"Mine know me." Sheep, you know, aren't very bright animals. You never see them doing tricks in circuses. Yet they actually do know their shepherd. Two flocks of them may be intermingled as they graze in a meadow or on a hillside. The shepherd of one flock calls out "Ya-hoo!" or something else in sheep language and immediately his sheep separate from the others. They don't, of course, know anything about their shepherd's character or intelligence, nor do they care about such things. But they do know the special sound of his voice, learned in a close and constant association with them. That voice they follow promptly and confidently, wherever he leads them. In the same way, the close association of a Superior with her subjects attaches them to her, makes them willing to follow her lead no matter whither. She does not remain aloof from them, in a sort of iron-lung isolation, but is ever "among them as one of them."

Why should you have a genuine love for your subjects? Because you have a genuine love for your Lord. And you prove your love for Him by your love for them. He made this point unmistakeably clear to Peter one day. He asked Peter, "Simon, son of John, lovest thou me?"

Peter, somewhat hurt by the question, answered, "Yea, Lord, thou knowest that I love thee."

Our Lord then told Peter how to prove his love: "Feed my lambs" (John 21:16). Saint Chrysostom rightly concludes: "To love God is to love neighbor." It's as uncomplicated as that.

How should you love your subjects? As God loves them. God sees not trees, as we do, but leaves: each leaf His creation, each leaf a masterpiece, and each leaf distinct from all other leaves. And He sees not humanity, as we do, but human beings: each His special creation, each made to His Own image and likeness, each unlike all other men, and each as supremely important as though he were the first and only man God had ever made. And God's love for men is no mere generic love ("I love mankind"), but an infinitely personal love ("I love *this* man and *that*"), expressing itself in His personal providence over each individual. Since no two men are alike, He treats no two alike. Nor does He make of them all the same demands—expecting from the man of one talent the same returns as from the man of five talents. He asks only that each man make the best use of his own gifts of nature and grace.

Of this same fabric must be your love of your subjects. It must be no academic, impersonal love which is hardly love at all, but a love that goes out to each subject individually, deals with each personally, watches over each singly, and reckons with the endowments of each separately. You must, as far as you can, take the place of the mother whom each of them left to enter the convent; the mother whose love, in its all-encompassing fulness, warmed and sheltered and comforted and cheered and enriched the life of each of them in her pre-convent years.

"I know mine." Do all—or even most—Superiors know theirs? Not according to a private survey I have conducted here and there among both men and women religious. Listen to some of their answers. "We wish," writes a teaching Brother, "our Superiors knew us, regarded us as people, not as mere cogs in a machine." "We wish," writes a religious priest, "our Superiors would think less about the community debt and more about the community." "Superiors," writes a nun, "could disarm a subject and forestall a 'situation' very often by a friendly greeting. Most Sisters of my acquaintance agree that Superiors are generally cold and unconcerned when the subjects have serious trouble." "The basic fault of many Superiors," writes another nun, "is their failure to recognize the individuality of each subject. Sisters complain, break silence, disobey, because they are trying to fill the void created by a Superior's lack of interest in them and coldness towards them. I know of another type of Superior who has a collection of our most difficult cases. She has them eating out of her hand because she makes them feel like people instead of inanimate objects." Now, I want to assure you that the religious quoted or to be quoted later are not malcontents. If they were, I'd have tossed their comments into the wastebasket.

I beg you, dear Sister, please, please, take a personal interest in each of your subjects, for God's sake and theirs. I plead strongly because I plead for something that is, alas, done far too rarely. Make each of your subjects feel that she really counts, really belongs. Show her that you *are* her mother and she *is* your daughter. When she comes to you for anything, receive her cordially and graciously; asking her not, "What do you want, Sister?" but, "What can I do for you, Sister?" There's a chasmic difference, you know, between those two questions. Listen to her problems with interest and empathy, never glancing at the clock no matter how diffuse her speech. Your time is God's time, and you cannot spend it better than in His interest. Have a motherly concern for the physical welfare of your subjects not less than for their spiritual; to the extent (suggests one of my nun prompters) of telling a Sister when her case warrants it: "Sister, I have noticed for several days you don't look well. Why not have supper early and get to bed for a good night's rest?"

Speaking of the physical welfare of subjects, I want to recall to you a tender episode from the life of Our Lord. It occurred one day at Capharnaum. The Apostles had just returned from their very first missionary journey. They gathered about Christ and eagerly "told Him all they had done"— as eagerly as little boys telling their father about their first youthful victory on a baseball diamond. Christ, smiling, nodding approval, listened to one of them after another. But He noticed that under their glow of enthusiasm there were lines of tiredness. So He invited them to go off with Him to some "quiet place"—as the Knox Version reads—"and rest a while": to some grove perhaps, or some hilltop retreat away from the crowds, where they could enjoy "time off" in a sort of family outing. Such was His considerateness towards them.

How well it would be if Sister Superiors had a like concern for the physical well-being of their hard-worked subjects! How well if on an occasional spring or autumn holiday they arranged an excursion for their Sisters to some "quiet place" in God's glorious countryside! How well if in summertime they sent their Sisters off for several weeks' vacation at some secluded seaside or lakeside cottage, where they could bask in the sun, and swim if they wanted, and go boating, and fish, and get rid of ghostly complexions and (a few of them) of ghastly complexes! The cottage rent would be money well invested. And how well if, on a winter holiday, instead of frantically cleaning convents already as immaculate as hospital surgical quarters, the Sisters were told to "rest a while," to relax, to recreate! All of them would be so much happier and so much healthier.

In a recent conference attended by one of my confreres, a group of Catholic surgeons, neurologists, and psychiatrists expressed unanimous alarm at the increasing number of Sisters in poor health. The doctors blamed two causes: 1) the excessive clothing worn by many Sisterhoods; 2) the lack of fresh air and outdoor exercise. No fool to rush in where angels fear to tread, I offer no comment about the clothing. (I have often wondered to myself, though, how Sisters can sit, all swathed and swaddled almost like mummies, in hot summerschool classrooms and hot summertime retreats with the patient resignation of Saint Lawrence sizzling on his gridiron. Their wrappings may not promote their health, but they certainly ought to promote their holiness.)

Yet from all I see and hear, the doctors are right about the Sisters' lack of air and exercise. How terribly intramural your life is! You move in the morning from convent to school; you move in the afternoon from school to convent. That's your day. A day off means a day in—in a convent filled maybe with the odor of cabbage cooking. Many Sisters in city convents, as you well know, have no convent yard to walk in, and the Sisters are forbidden to walk anywhere else. Some Sisterhoods frown (and they can really frown!) on all outdoor sports for their Sisters—horseshoe pitching, volley ball, tennis, handball, basketball, even if indulged in behind high convent garden walls. And I've seen Sisters' novitiates on country estates, completely isolated, far from the vulgar gaze, where the beautiful tile swimming-pools installed by the original owners of the estates have not seen a toe ripple their waters since the Sisters took over.

Now, if this attitude doesn't smack of Jansenism, then I, for one, don't know what does. Are air and water and exercise inherently evil things, so that any partiality towards them bespeaks moral depravity? Are they threats to a religious vocation, so that any dalliance with them invites apostasy? If so, then poor Francis of Assisi—that lover of sun and moon and wind and woods and streams and all living things—must have been, as he claimed to be, the worst of sinners. At least he scandalously lacked custody of the eyes. To say nothing about his total lack of a sense of religious decorum—he roaming woods, talking to birds, or singing blithe songs to the accompaniment of his make-believe violin! How, I wonder, did he ever manage to get canonized?

I have forgotten the name of a book that Father Barry O'Neill, C.S.C., wrote for Sisters years ago, but I remember it was a fine book. And I remember that a long chapter in it fulminated, with all the holy wrath of Jeremias the Prophet, against Sisters' neglect of their health and of the physical exercise necessary to promote their health. Father quoted authorities ancient and modern, he piled up statistics upon statistics, he forged iron syllogism after syllogism. And he ended by shaking an angry finger and saying in effect: "Sister, thou shalt not kill—and that prohibition includes suicide!" To which dictum, closing my own comments on the topic, I say heartily, "Amen!"

To retrace our steps: you as Superior must be a loving mother to each of your subjects. And you must be a mother to all of them without exception. Some, admittedly, are more likeable, because they are more congenial, responsive, and cooperative; yet all are your daughters. You must imitate the mother of a family of eleven who, when asked which of them was her favorite, answered: "My favorite? Oh, the one that's sick, till he gets well; the one that's away, till he comes back." You must flee, as a plague, any inordinate attachment to any of your subjects.

If Our Lord asked you, "Sister, lovest thou Me?" you would answer, probably in the aggrieved tone of Peter, "Yea, Lord, Thou knowest that I love Thee." Then He would impose on you the self-same proof that He imposed on Peter that far-off day in a far-off land: "Feed my sheep—feed my sheep."

Your affectionate uncle,

FATHER C.

10. "*Charity is Kind*"

DEAR SISTER,

This letter, as you will see in a moment, is really a continuation of the one that preceded it. That one dealt with motherly affection; this one will deal with kindness, which is merely the outward sign of that inward grace. "Charity is kind," wrote Saint Paul. Why this theme again? Because no matter what other commendable traits you have as a Superior, if you lack kindness you are, as the same Saint Paul says unequivocally, just plain "nothing."

In a metallic echo of Saint Paul, the French Sulpician, Father J. Guibert, declares: "You . . . who flatter yourself that you possess God, and yet are pitiless, unkind, harsh, I say to you that your so-called religiousness is an illusion; for as long as kindness is not in you, God is not with you." Vehement words? Yes, but no more vehement than Our Lord's condemnation of the Pharisees—who, be it remembered, were religious Superiors. He, Who readily forgave Magdalen and Peter and Dismas and His murderers, heaped fearful scorn on the Pharisees. "Blind guides," He called them, "whited sepulchres . . . a generation of vipers"—because they were unjust and unkind.

Father Faber, himself a religious, wrote that "religious are an unkind lot." Religious, he explained, are so busy with their poverty and chastity and obedience that they are prone to overlook or underrate so inconspicuous a virtue as kindness. And who will contradict him? There *are* religious—more than a few—who are exemplary in their observance of the religious vows, their practice of religious self-denial, their fidelity to a religious schedule, their fulfillment of religious duties, who are yet unkind. And lacking kindness they are the Foolish Virgins, declares Saint Augustine, with no oil in their lamps.

Kindness, like culture, is hard to define, though all of us know it when we meet it. Kindness is "an overflowing of self upon others," said Faber, who wrote such eloquent conferences on it. Kindness puts others in our place, treating them as we should like to be treated. Kindness is a giving when we are not required to give, or not even expected to give. And not just a giving, but a gracious giving. Kindness is the good manners of charity. If as a Christmas gift, for instance, your Uncle Tom wanted to give you a pair of black stockings ("Please, Uncle Tom, be sure they're cotton!"), he might simply hand them to you unwrapped, saying, "Merry Christmas, Sister!" Well, that would be charity. On the other hand, though, he might enclose them in a Christmas box, insert a Christmas card with a personal message on it, wrap the box in silver paper and tie it with a red ribbon. That would be kindness. And such kindness would make the gift seem twice a gift.

Kindness is the full bloom and fragrance of charity. It's charity with a smile that puts others at their ease. A Sister at Saint Gervase's, needing new shoes, asks permission for them from her Superior.

Her Superior frowns. "Well, all right, if you *must*," says the Dolorous Doler, "but don't think you have to buy the most expensive pair in the store!" Permission granted.

A Sister at Saint Protase's, needing new shoes, asks permission for them from her Superior.

Her Superior beams. "Why, surely, Sister," says the Generous Granter, "and be sure you get a good pair, none of those cheap things that can ruin your feet!" Permission granted.

It's the same permission in both cases, but how differently given! Didn't one of the poets say something about gifts losing all their worth "when givers prove unkind"?

Kindness is a quiet, unspectacular virtue. It's more, Faber observed, "the grass of the field than a cedar of Lebanon." The cedar of Lebanon, you know, is a mighty, towering, spreading tree that dominates all its surroundings. The birds find shelter and rest in it, but they cannot eat it. They find their food in the grass of the field. And how that grass clothes the field with a gentle beauty that gladdens the eye of man! In another figure, Guibert calls kindness "a wayside spring." Even in modern, mechanized America we occasionally come upon such a spring in the hills, a pipe jutting from the rocks and running cold, clear water, with a sign announcing, "Approved for Drinking." On hot days many tourists stop, quench their thirst, go their way with spirits refreshed. The spring gives to all, yet asks nothing in return. If it could talk it would say, "Please, no need to thank me. It's my privilege!"

Let's leave the grass of the field and the wayside spring, and take a close look at the kind Superior in action. She has a cheerful greeting for everyone she meets. Like the Mother General described in my previous letter, a kind Superior scatters words of praise and encouragement liberally among her subjects. She agrees with Monsignor Gay that to withhold deserved compliments "is nothing but Jansenism, a heresy that would destroy nature." There are, she knows, few Saint Pauls who can truthfully exclaim, in utter contempt of human opinion, "Henceforth let no man be troublesome to me" (Gal. 6:17). She knows the young, in the groping beginnings of religious life, would lose heart over their blunders if she didn't encourage them with wholesome praise. She knows the middle-aged, weary of well-doing and palled by the monotony of convent life, need the stimulus of new responsibilities and appreciation for their carrying them. She knows the old, in their steadily shrinking world of acquaintances and activities, need desperately a little notice and considerateness to rally their hope and strength. A kind Superior knows that if she praises her subjects in one thing, they will do their best in everything. She has no fear at all that a compliment, well deserved, will go to her subjects' heads; she is sure it will, rather, go to their hearts, warming them to a greater love of God and a greater zeal for His glory.

I know a religious priest who has worked for years collecting funds to support the foreign missions of his Congregation. How hard he works is indicated by the sum of money he collects annually almost single-handed—some sixty thousand dollars. I once visited his working quarters, listened to him explain in detail his equipment and his mode of operation, and complimented him cordially on his signal success. He thanked me, and added with a rather pathetic sigh: "I just wish my Superior General appreciated that success a little bit. He lives here on this same corridor, but in five years he has never once stepped into this office to see how things are going. All he does is take the checks, with a grunt, and toss them into his desk drawer." I expect that priest will be amazed when, arriving in the next world, he will hear Our Lord say, "Well done, faithful servant!" Surely, he never heard anything like that in *this* world!

Dear Sister, please don't take your subjects for granted. Notice them, take interest in their work, praise them, compliment them, encourage them. Kind words cost you nothing but a little breath. Though they do not in the least impoverish you, how incalculably they enrich the lives of your subjects! One kind word can strengthen and heal like a sacrament. It can lighten a burden that was becoming almost too heavy for human shoulders. It can sweeten a cup of sorrow almost too bitter for human lips. It can give new will to one on the verge of settling into fatal torpor. It can give new hope to one sinking into despair. It can spark with new energy one worn out by toil. It can summon to useful purpose latent powers for good that otherwise would atrophy. It can steady vocations that were slipping. It can make friends out of foes, saints out of cynics. And it's so easily, so very easily, spoken. Let kind words be your vocabulary. They are, in Faber's famed saying, "the music of the world." And in this music you can, with no conservatory training at all, be a great artist if you but will.

Next, see how the kind Superior has time for all her subjects. She lends a patient ear to her subjects' recitals of their woes, though the recitals are oft-repeated and lackluster performances. She knows that troubled people find relief in telling their troubles; so she lets her subjects talk freely, without unnecessary interruptions. If she cannot solve all their troubles, she can at least sympathize with them.

In the further interest of kindness, a Superior can take a hint from Saint Pius X. When seminary rector at Treviso, and known as Monsignor Sarto, he occasionally had to set out early in the morning to fulfill preaching engagements in Padua or Venice. An old houseman had the duty of waking him on those mornings. With lantern in hand, the old man would stand down the corridor, quietly waiting till the tower-clock struck three. Then he would promptly go to the Monsignor's door, knock, listen till he heard the Monsignor call from within, "Thank you for wakening me." Then the old man would shuffle off, feeling proud and pleased with his fulfillment of so important a duty. What he never knew was that, long before he came, the Monsignor had been awake and up, but had put out his light at the old man's approach. Just so does the kind Superior accept little services of which she really has no need—to allow her subjects the joy of being kind to her.

Consider how the kind Superior gives orders. She never commands in a dictatorial tone, as though she were a prison matron barking at her sullen charges. Rather, as Saint Alphonsus urges, she uses polite, oblique language, more as though requesting a favor than issuing a command: "Would you mind . . . If you please . . . I'd appreciate it if . . ." and the like. Thus her subjects obey gladly, measuring up to the courteous treatment accorded them. Belloc says that "the grace of God is in courtesy." So is the winning of friends and the influencing of people. To the meek has the earth been promised. Nowhere does Scripture give permission to do violence to anyone, to insult anyone, to rule anyone ruthlessly. "Put up again thy sword back into its place," Christ told Peter; "for all that take up the sword shall perish with the sword" (Matt. 26:52).

Of course, a kind Superior does—and must—rule her convent, but she does so without harshness or "bitter zeal." Her rule of strength tempered by kindness does not cramp, much less does it crush. As Saint Vincent de Paul quickly discovered in his first dealings with convicts, force hurts everything it touches. "When I spoke harshly to them," he confesses, "I spoilt everything. But when I praised them for being resigned to their hard lot, when I kissed their chains and showed them I felt for them, then they listened to me and gave glory to God, and sought to put themselves into the state of grace."

Saint Bonaventure admirably summarizes the case: "Since it is not possible to please everyone, it is advisable to err rather on the side of kindness, the Superior winning for himself the affection of his subjects, who will in consequence fall in more readily with his suggestions, will have recourse to him more confidently in their needs, and will more readily imitate him. His position alone should be enough to ensure for him all necessary respect: to add thereto an austere severity is only to make himself 'impossible' as far as ordinarily diffident people are concerned."

Finally, the kind Superior shows concern especially for any sick Sister: whether one abed with serious illness, or one crippled though able to move about, or one weak from old age or a frail constitution. All such need whatever medical attention can help them. They likewise need dispensations concerning food, clothing, choir-attendance; and exemptions from normal duties within and without the convent. And all such need much kindness. Perhaps one subject *is* something of a hypochondriac; therefore are all claiming sickness hypochondriacs? Perhaps one *is* incurable. In that case, says Saint Bonaventure, "the more hopeless the disease, the more splendid is the devotion and unselfish the charity of those who strive to alleviate it." He adds pointedly that it would be "an excellent thing" for Superiors to have passed through a period of poor health themselves, so that they might learn sympathy for the sick.

Kindness to the sick consists in more than temperature-taking, medicine-measuring, tray-carrying: it consists also in words of comfort, inquiries about the sick one's condition and wants, assurances of prayer. General Patton, tough Commander of the Third Army in Europe during World War II, would take time out, even during battle, to see that dry socks went out to troops on the battle-line, to direct new methods of preventing trench feet, to kneel in mud aiding the wounded till an ambulance came. Well, if that happened "in the dry wood"—a layman, what should happen "in the green wood"—a religious?

Oh, kindness can be a hard assignment: especially when your sinus is acting up, or your nerves are frayed, or you're bone-weary from work, or you're discouraged by some failure; or when your subjects prove thoughtless or foolish or ignorant. But it is so very necessary. For, remember, "charity is kind," and without charity. . . .

Your affectionate uncle,

FATHER C.

11. "All are One

DEAR SISTER:

"Mirror, mirror on the wall, who's the fairest one of all?" asked Snow White's ugly and cruel stepmother, and angrily refused to accept the mirror's answer that she *wasn't*. Such was her self-love. The same self-love prompts us to opine that the one we see in the mirror is, well, if not the fairest one of all, certainly fair enough. Maybe our looks would win no prize in a beauty contest; but, ah, it's character that counts, particularly after forty-five. "All the glory of the king's daughter is within" (Ps. 44:14).

In our mirror we see a character not without its little blemishes (whose is?) but containing just about the right ingredients: intelligence, good sense, integrity, a fine self-command, a delightful sense of humor, a broad charity towards our fellowmen. Our tastes are sound, our views are sane. Seldom do we question them; never do we ridicule them. We rarely make mistakes, and then only when mistakes are humanly unavoidable. We are truly satisfactory people. If our neighbors were like us, they, too, would be truly satisfactory people. We could love them spontaneously; we could live with them harmoniously. But, alas, they are not like us. They differ from us on a dozen counts: perhaps in nationality, color, age; certainly in appearance, temperament, habits, opinions, likes and dislikes. The less they differ from us, the more likely will they become our friends; the more they differ from us, the more likely will they become our foes.

The differences between them and us frankly annoy us. If marked or persistent, they may even infuriate us. What can we do about them? Obviously, we cannot remake all our neighbors according to our own image and likeness. We can do one of two things: liquidate those who differ from us—and that is the Soviet solution; or tolerate them,—and that is the Christian solution. "Bear ye one another's burdens," Saint Paul expresses it, "and thus ye shall fulfill the law of Christ" (Gal. 6:12).

These words of Saint Paul, you know, are read aloud by the priest during a Catholic marriage ceremony. It is safe to say that nine times out of ten, though, the bride and groom, wrapped in their own thoughts and emotions, don't hear these words at all; or that if they do hear them, they are totally unimpressed by this talk about "one another's burdens." Why, they are the perfect match, and they know it! But see them a year later at the breakfast table. He sits munching toast behind the sports page of the morning paper; she sits munching toast behind the society page. They exchange not a word, not even a glance. They just munch. The perfect match? They look like the perfect mismatch! What has happened to them in one year? They have come to know each other, that's all. Their courtship should have been a time of mutual self-revelation; instead, it was a time of mutual deception. During it they wore masks, spoke actors' lines, smiled endearingly and postured charmingly. After the honeymoon, when they settled down to the matter-of-fact business of living together, each found that he or she had married no angel at all but an ordinary human being with some very irritating moods, habits, opinions, tastes; and with faults, says Phyllis McGinley, marked as plainly as towels, *His, Hers*. To live together in anything resembling happiness, they must learn to live with each other's differences and faults: they must "bear one another's burdens." If they don't, they will become another melancholy divorce statistic under the familiar heading of "incompatibility."

In the same way, and for the same reasons, it is hard for

religious of different ages, temperaments, backgrounds, likes and dislikes to live together within the walls of a convent. God declared that "it is not good for man to be alone" (Gen. 2:18), and He provided life-long companionship for man by instituting marriage. To help the married couple to live together, His Son supernaturalized their union by making it a grace-laden sacrament. But the union of us religious is no such sacramental union. We didn't even choose one another as companions; our Major Superior joined us together, "for better or for worse." It would be strange, then, if our togetherness didn't create problems sometimes and challenge our mutual forbearance at all times.

To begin with, there are the personal differences. One religious is phlegmatic, another is choleric; one is talkative, another is reticent; one laughs much, another laughs little; one is strict in views, another is liberal; one likes windows open, another likes them closed. In fact, I've often thought what an enlightening experience it would be (but so hazardous as never to be indulged in) if at recreation some evening each member of a community—say, of yours—took pencil and paper, wrote at the top, "Things I Wish My Sisters Wouldn't Do," listed the names of all her convent companions, then went into wishful details. A typical paper might read something like this:

PRIMA—I wish that, if she can't sleep, she'd let the rest of us sleep and not lumber around in her room like a sick elephant.

SECUNDA—I wish that she'd clear her throat before she reads the meditation, and not sound like a ventriloquist with tonsilitis.

TERTIA—I wish that, just once, she'd keep on pitch during the Office.

QUARTA—I wish that she wouldn't dawdle with her breakfast, holding up the rest of us.

QUINTA—I wish that she didn't make such a production of straightening her room after breakfast, banging the push-broom against the radiator.

SEXTA—I wish that, when she teaches, she didn't shout like a sea captain giving orders through a gale.

SEPTIMA—I wish that she'd control her students during recess, and not leave it to me to stop their fights.

OCTAVA—I wish that, like the rest of us, she straightened her classroom window-shades before she leaves school.

NONA—I wish that at supper she'd stop quoting those "bright sayings" of her kindergarten children.

DECIMA—I wish that at recreation she'd play something besides those Montovani records with their meowing strings.

And more and more of the same. Each Sister, if apprised of the ways in which she pin-pricks the others, would ask in amazement, "Do I do those things?"—quite confident, of course, that she doesn't.

Inevitably, the smaller the convent, the more constant are the pin-pricks, and the more constant is the need of mutual forbearance. In a small rectory resided two religious priests: the pastor, in his sixties, as round, unsmiling and incommunicative as Buddha; the assistant, in his twenties, genial, out-going, and conversational. The pastor insisted that, in addition to praying and eating together, they recreated together ("Remember, we're still community men"). This meant that together they sat down before the TV set. In five minutes, the paunchy pastor was asleep and snoring. He snored through program after program. Eventually, yawning, the assistant would tiptoe off to bed; but not to sleep—for the TV blared on and on, "vexing the drowsy ear of night" till it lost its voice at sign-off time. Now, religious togetherness doesn't demand all this. It doesn't demand that we sit on one another's lap. It doesn't demand that we have no respite from one another. "The more intimate a family circle," writes Phyllis McGinley, "the more fresh air and mental breathing-space that circle should enclose. The human animal needs a freedom seldom mentioned. He needs a little privacy quite as much as he wants understanding, vitamins, exercise, or praise."

It's sound psychology, I'm sure, that you should allow your Sisters as much privacy as their schedule permits: that, for instance, you let them study alone before or after they recreate together. "Let each be master of his time till eight," Lady Macbeth wisely told her early-arrived guests, "to make society the sweeter." The considerable togetherness of convent life, to be at all tolerable, cries out for considerable apartness. Absence, you know, makes the heart grow fonder, while perpetual presence can paralyze its beat.

Then there are the differences between your young Sisters and your old. Wide differences they are indeed; May has so little in common with December. The young like noise and activity; the old, quiet and repose. The young resent advice; the old insist on trying to impart it. The young are keen on exercise; the old consider it wasted energy. The young equate change with progress; the old equate change with heresy. The young are full of great expectations and golden prophecies; the old are, said Horace, "praisers of the bygone days" when they were young. How hard for them to regard each other with a kindly eye! And how hard for a Superior to deal effectively with both of them!

The young want activity: give it to them. Give them plenty of work and responsibility, to utilize their vibrant energy. Let them make suggestions, let them tackle new projects, let them learn by doing, succeed by failing. And please let them recreate in ways involving more physical exercise than checkers or knitting.

The old, because of their long years in the community, are inclined to confuse their age with Superiorship. They may need at times to be reminded gently who has the authority. They find obedience harder with each year. Ease it for them by your affability and your thoughtfulness towards them. This point recalls an incident from the ex-nun's biography that I quoted in a previous letter. In a convent mentioned in that book, the custom was to have common spiritual reading immediately after school. Some of the old Sisters, exhausted after the day's grind, would nod during the reading. The Superior would sharply call out the name of a nodding Sister, tell her to repeat what had just been read—confusing the poor old nun to tears, embarrassing her before all the young Sisters. (Whether the Superior then told her to write it a thousand times, wasn't stated.) That Superior, I submit, deserved a month in jail for her utter cruelty.

The old like to be consulted. Consult them, then, even if you can't always follow their advice. They need to feel that they still count in the community. So give them something to do within their capabilities, and compliment them for doing it. If they go on a trip, give them a generous purse, though they'll probably deplete it little. Listen with interest to their reminiscences about the old days: about Mother This who opened the convent in Centretown, and Mother That who added the wing to the novitiate; about the incredible hardships of convent life in those far-off days. If eventually you must end the epic, do it graciously, remembering that, as Saint Therese says, "there is so gracious a way of refusing what we cannot grant that the refusal pleases almost as much as the bestowal." And mark the birthdays and religious anniversaries of your old Sisters with a festal dinner and some little gift. Charity towards the old, like charity towards the dead, is charity pure and undefiled, with no alloy of self-seeking in it.

Then, finally, there are in religious life a few individuals whose singularity is so pronounced as to make them "problem children." There, for one, is Sister Lacrymosa, whose feast is the Feast of the Seven Dolors. She wears the air of a tragedy queen. She seems to cherish some great secret sorrow. Her nearest approach to language is ordinarily a sigh. As cheerfulness is an antiseptic, her gloom is a virus. You must watch that she doesn't spread that virus among her school children: with gruesome stories about a boy whose hand suddenly withered when raised to strike his father; about a girl who was struck by lightning immediately after her first bite into a wiener on a Friday picnic; about souls coming back from Purgatory to make restitution for money stolen from church poor-boxes; about a theatre roof's caving in on people watching a Grade-C movie. By such macabre tales she makes God a Monster in the minds of her children. Saint Teresa used to exclaim, "God deliver me from gloomy nuns!" A melancholy nun, she felt, could destroy the spirit and discipline of a whole convent. She must be dealt with firmly. She is self-willed; hence she must be kept under authority. Keep her busy, Saint Teresa prescribes. Shorten her prayers, curtail her fasts, and make her exercise in the fresh air.

There's also Sister Contraria. She's the one the retreat master met as he was about to leave her convent. "Sister," he told her, "I'd like to say good-bye to the Sister Superior."

Sister answered grimly, "So would I!"

Sister Contraria is a law unto herself. You can never be sure what she will say or do except that it will be the opposite of what everyone else says and does. Superiors are her fixed aversion. If the Superior is strict, Contraria demands, "Are we kindergarten children?" If the Superior is easy-going, Contraria calls her "Suspended Animation." To her, the household regulations are nonsense; reproofs are rank injustices. How did Contraria ever get that way? Maybe from a physical or a mental disorder. Or maybe her trouble is wounded pride or envy. How should you deal with her? Your first impulse will certainly be, to ask for her transfer to another convent: in the manner of a classmate of mine in the seminary who, grimacing, pushed his piece of pie across the table to me and said, "You take it; it upsets my stomach." To transfer the problem (Contraria) from convent to convent is to leave it still a problem.

Why not try to solve the problem? Why not try to take the wind out of Contraria's sails by agreeing with her that, unquestionably, "the world *is* out of joint"—particularly that part of it covered by your Institute and your own convent. Then blandly ask her what she would suggest "to set it right." Maybe she will find it easier to describe ailments than to prescribe cures. At all events, overwhelm her with kindness. If that doesn't change her, well, try to bear patiently with her. It must be in the plans of God's Providence that she is there with you: to further by her imperfection the perfection of the rest of you, as a dull whet-stone sharpens instruments held against it.

Despite all our differences, we are to be, Saint Paul insists, "all one." How can such perfect unity be achieved? Only, Saint Paul significantly continues, "in Christ." Only when our hearts have caught from the Sacred Heart of Christ a charity that makes us forget ourselves and think constantly of others, a charity that makes us overlook the natural differences that divide us and stress the supernatural ties that bind us.

Your affectionate uncle,

FATHER C.

12. *"In the Spirit of Meekness"*

Dear Sister,

I second your motion. There ought to be a book, or at least a booklet, entitled *The Art of Correcting.* As you say, many religious Superiors could use it. So could many more parents and teachers. The word "art" in the title would be apposite; for effective correction calls for consummate technique. It's like surgery: done deftly, it can save lives; done crudely, it can lose them.

Why is art requisite? Because of human pride, self-love, self-esteem. Most men are kin to the Negro who diagnosed himself to his minister as "not exactly a good man, Reverend, but what you might call a respectable sinner." Most men, even condemned criminals, feel they have in them some vestiges of respectability, and resent any reminder to the contrary. Just as "men must be taught as though you taught them not," they must be corrected as though you corrected them not. The therapy must be well nigh painless or they will fight it; and their "last state will be worse than their first."

For what transgressions must you correct your subjects? Certainly not for the inevitable "seven-times-daily" falls of even the just; not for minor transgressions committed in ignorance or thoughtlessness. "It is indeed the mark of a level-headed man," writes Saint Bonaventure, "to weigh things as they are, good or bad, and not, like some foolish people, to think little at times and to magnify the trivial, judging motes to be beams, straining out gnats and swallowing the camels. A neglected bow in choir elicits a far more heated reproof than long uncharitable conversations about the brethren: a wrong versicle recited or some little rubric omitted raises a far greater storm of indignation than a real scandal."

A prudent Superior knows what to overlook. She realizes that neither her own corruptible nature nor that of her subjects will don incorruptibility on this side of the grave. So she tries to follow the advice of the old couplet:

> Be to their virtues very kind,
> And to their faults a little blind.

The only alternative to being "a little blind" is to see everything, and to assume the role of a neurotic mother who nags her children from dawn to dark: "Billie, stop pounding that piano! Betty, keep out of that closet! Billie, stop that whistling! Betty, let those curtains alone! Billie, stop beating that drum!" She might as well tell them, "Stop breathing!" What good does her nagging do? By italicizing everything, it emphasizes nothing. It soon degenerates into a sort of radio static, audible but meaningless. Unlike such a mother, the sensible Superior seldom raises her voice. She lives and lets live. Since most of the irregularities of her subjects are trivial, she ignores them, calmly accepting the general thesis that, despite all the good will in the world, both she and her subjects are certain to prove on occasion "a little less than the angels."

A serious transgression, however, you definitely must correct, for the good of the transgressor and for the good of the community. By your very office you are obliged to "keep watch, as having to render an account" of the souls entrusted to your care (Hebr. 13:17). The priest Heli, you remember, kept no such watch over his sons. "His eyes were grown dim"—and so, apparently, were his wits. He knew that his sons were stealing from the altar and were waylaying women who came to the Temple to pray. He knew that their scandalous conduct was bringing the worship of God into disrepute. Yet his only correction of them was the bloodless plea: "Do not so, my sons: for it is no good report that I hear" (I Kings 2:24). And "because he knew that his sons did wickedly, and did not chastise them," by divine decree both he and his sons met a violent death. Surely a caution, this, to the Superior who shirks her duty to correct a gravely delinquent subject.

Saint Bonaventure lists three grades of transgressors. First are those who, having transgressed, promptly repent. Correct such, he urges, "in the spirit of meekness, lest thou also be tempted" (Gal. 6:1). Second are those who, having transgressed, attempt to conceal or minimize or defend their transgressions. Treat such, he urges, as Christ treated Judas: silently tolerating the fault as long as, hidden, it does no public harm; openly correcting the fault if it develops to such proportions as to be visible to others. Third are those who transgress grievously, publicly, repeatedly, contumaciously. For the general good, he insists, dismiss such. He quotes Saint Paul: "Put away the evil one from among you" (I Cor. 5:13). But do so, he adds, only after much prayer, deliberation, and consultation.

In all cases, you must approach the task of correction with an open mind. No one, in religious life as in secular life, is guilty of wrong-doing until proven guilty. It's humanly possible, you know, that you've misinterpreted a Sister; that you've misread sickness for indolence or ignorance for disobedience or shyness for uncooperativeness or zeal for brashness. Or it's possible you've received a distorted report on her from one who is scrupulous or envious or even calumnious. After all, Christ was unjustly accused—and unjustly sentenced. And so have been more than one religious in the long annals of Christ's Church. Justice dictates, therefore, that, after you've stated the charge against a Sister, you let her answer the charge if she can. Hear her out. "Before thou inquire," Sacred Scripture rules, "blame no man" (Ecclus. 19:1).

All right, then: say that such an inquiry has clearly proven a Sister guilty, and hence the correction of her necessary. Remember that the first canon of the art of correction is timeliness. Ecclesiastes notes that "all things have their season," including "a time to keep silence, and a time to speak" (Eccles. 3:1,7). Surely, it would be ruinous timing to berate a Sister who is utterly exhausted from work or is suffering from a migrane headache or is crushed by some tragic news from home. It would be ruthlessly inappropriate to sentence her on a Christmas or an Easter, turning for her, and probably for the community at large, a white "day the Lord hath made" into a black "day of wrath." Most important of all, it would be calamitous ill-timing to correct in anger, when your reason is out of focus and your speech is out of control. Can you possibly "be angry and sin not"? or may you not act and speak so intemperately, so unjustly, that you will have matter for regret for the rest of your days?

It would be just as untimely to correct a Sister when she herself is agitated. Saint Alphonsus writes: "The correction must be deferred till her anger has subsided, else we should only increase her indignation"—should heap new coals on the fire. Surely, in all these and similar circumstances, the correction can wait a day or more, until a calmer atmosphere is more apt to make it beneficial.

Charity, of course, requires that you correct a private offence privately. "If thy brother shall offend against thee, go, and rebuke him between thee and him alone" (Matt. 18:15). I heard somewhere of a seminary rector who once summoned to his office the deacon class on the eve of their ordination to the priesthood. After surveying them in dramatic silence for a while, he announced: "One of you will be ordained tomorrow against my vote. He is an utterly unfit candidate for the priesthood. I will wager that he will not last in the priesthood one year." A tremor of dismay ran through the group, each deacon wondering, "Is it I?" Slowly the rector pointed a finger at one of them. "You are the one," he said. "Mark my word: you will not last one year!" With that dire prophecy, he dismissed the group.

What conceivable purpose did that public exposure serve? It certainly didn't help in any way the man exposed. It filled the minds of his classmates with a hundred sinister surmises. It cast a pall of leaden gloom over the ordination of them all. Merely that and nothing more.

Both charity and justice, I say, demand that the correction of a private trespass be private. Whatever else a subject might lose by her private offence, including even the grace of God, she does *not* lose the right to her good name. Her Superior must respect that right. She must not expose to public view a subject's private transgression—nor turn it into a conversation-piece at home or abroad. Common sense, too, demands such private treatment. Why harangue the whole community because one member of it has missed chapel or overstayed an out-permission or made purchases without permissions? One has erred; only one should be corrected.

Another important consideration to bear in mind is that circumstances alter cases. Woodrow Wilson wrote: "All the bindings of our libraries do not contain the various world of circumstance." Nor do all the bindings of our religious Rules and Constitutions reckon with the differences between one religious and another. The Superiors must do that. Here, for instance, is a young Sister fresh from the novitiate; of great good will, but still ignorant of many of the customs of the community. She must be taught, rather than reprimanded for her errors. Or here is another recently professed Sister who, before entering religion, had a good position, made good money, dressed well, owned a car, traveled widely, enjoyed an occasional dance or cocktail party. Short of a repetition of the miraculous and instantaneous conversion of Saul of Tarsus, she will need time to acclimate herself completely to religious poverty, obedience, simplicity, mortification. She should not be treated, then, as though she were a peasant girl from the Brazilian hinterland, for whom the austerities of convent life would be undreamed-of luxuries. To deal intelligently with your subjects, you have to use not a ruler but a slide-rule. You have to treat each as the individual that nature, grace, environment, education, and habits have made of each of them. And that, I admit, is quite a large order.

In a park in Boston there stands a life-sized statue of a surgeon performing an operation in pre-anaesthetic times (Boston was, I believe, the birthplace of anaesthesia). The hapless adult male patient, standing with each arm gripped by a gargantuan orderly, has the wildly agonized look of a figure in the Laocoon Group, while the grimly determined surgeon incises him. Modern anaesthesia, thank heaven and Boston, has benignly changed that picture. Today the patient of surgery, after an anaesthetic, is blissfully insensate to the surgeon's scalpel.

Now, no Superior, correcting a subject, can make the operation entirely painless. Still, by first administering an injection of praise, she can greatly reduce the subject's pain. The Superior, I mean, can first cite some laudable trait, some worthy accomplishment, of the subject, predisposing the subject for the touch of the knife: "I hear fine reports, Sister, about your work in the classroom (or office, or laboratory, or hospital wards), but I'm somewhat worried about your temper (or critical attitude, or disregard of regulations, or association with seculars)." An absurdly refined approach? Hardly so; for according to the Apocalypse it was God's Own approach in correcting the Bishop of Ephesus in the early Church: "I know thy works, and thy labor, and thy patience . . . . But I have somewhat against thee, because thou hast left thy first charity" (Apoc. 2:2,4). So went also the corrections of the

Bishop of Smyrna, the Bishop of Pergamus, the Bishop of Thyatira: first the commendation, then the correction—a sugar-coating of the bitter pill.

In summary, be sure the correction you give is deserved by the seriousness of the offence and by the subject's proven guilt. Be sure that it is timely: never when the subject is unwell, exhausted, or dejected; never when either of you is angry. Be sure that it is administered privately for a private offence. But, above all, be sure that you correct kindly. After all, your delinquent subject has offended not *you,* but God. "The bent reed He does not break"—He straightens it to grow anew; "the smoking flax He does not quench"—He fans it to new flame. Your purpose in correction is "not to destroy souls," with words of ridicule or sarcasm that sting like asps. You have no warrant to humiliate or hurt anybody. No, "not to destroy souls, but to save"—to pour the wine and oil of the Good Samaritan into wounds and to bind them with healing kindness. You may be sure that if kind correction doesn't lead your errant subject to reprimand and improve herself, nothing else will.

Said the wise Catherine the First of Russia, "I praise loudly, I blame softly." Which wraps up in a neat little package almost everything I have been trying to tell you in this lengthy letter.

Your affectionate uncle,

FATHER C.

13. *"I Also am Subject to Authority"*

Dear Sister,

You ask me to "say something about obedience." The request reminds me of a request some nuns made of a confrere of mine known for his Irish wit: "Father, say something funny!" Both requests, I mean, are a bit generic. I *have,* you know, said something about obedience under other headings. I urged you to keep intact the regular discipline, to give few orders but clear ones, to make your commands sound more like requests than commands.

Concerning the obedience you extract from your subjects, I can think of only one point to add. There is, as you are aware, a solemn command known as a "formal obedience." In issuing it, the Superior uses some such explicit phrase as "I command you under holy obedience." Our appointments as friars, for example, come to us in that august form—in letters called "Obediences," signed by our Provincial and sealed with the seal of our Province. They impose upon us a grave obligation to go to the appointed friary and do the appointed work. To disobey them would be to sin mortally.

In the running of your convent, you too are empowered to impose, for a serious reason, this formal obedience on your subjects. But be sure that the reason is serious, critically so. Be sure that you have previously exhausted, in all charity and patience, every other available means to win compliance with your orders. For this formal obedience may swiftly and tidily solve your own problems, but it can create well nigh insoluble problems for your subjects. It hangs the Sword of Damacles over their heads: the constant and harrowing threat of mortal sin if ever in their proven human weakness they disobey your command. And that, dear Sister, is not something you should do lightly.

I have asked many male religious Superiors how often they have imposed this obedience on their subjects. Some of these Superiors have had true "problem children"; yet their unanimous answer has been, "Never." They tried, instead, to follow Saint Paul's advice: "An ancient man, rebuke not, but entreat him as a father; young men, as brethren" (I Tim. 5:1). For they know that, whether the offendor is ancient or young, such "holy obedience" is the ultimate, extreme measure, one step removed from dismissal. It's a kind of religious martial law, with a shoot-to-kill order against any transgressor. I trust that in your tenure of office you will find less drastic means to resolve your serious problems, if you have any.

When dealing with ordinary transgressions, watch that your language doesn't create false impressions about their gravity. If you say, "Sister, you have broken the Great Silence three times," Sister, if young and not very bright, may panic and conclude she has broken a vow or two and all of the Ten Commandments. Actually, she's broken a disciplinary regulation involving no sin in itself at all. Or if you say, "Sister, our holy Constitutions do not permit lisle gloves, such as you are wearing," Sister may think herself an apostate from the community; whereas the Constitutions do not make sinful even the wearing of boxing gloves. You want Sister's conscience, I'm sure, to be formed according to the norms of your Institute, but not to be misinformed.

The obedience you ask me to discuss is, I take it, your own obedience, not that of your subjects. What, though, is there to tell you? You already know that, like the centurion in the Gospel, you too are "subject to authority" (Matt. 8:9): to Rome, to your Mother Provincial, to your Rule and Constitutions, to your bishop in certain diocesan matters, to your pastor in certain school matters. You are by no means—though your subjects may enviously think so—your own boss.

I imagine you have often heard religious obedience described as an all-out surrender, made for the love of God, of one's will and judgment to the will and judgment of a lawful religious Superior. I have often described it so myself on retreats, explaining that after this surrender a religious becomes in effect a marionette, with his movements operated by someone literally above. If understood rightly, this definition passes muster. But sometimes it is not understood rightly. Some religious object: "If I give up my judgment and will, how is it that, if I no longer have them, they still assert themselves?" Well, we are here not using strictly literal language. Getting rid of one's will by the vow of obedience isn't like getting rid of one's appendix. The removed appendix will never again cause trouble. But after the vow of obedience we still retain the judgment and will we possessed before the vow. Maybe a more accurate description of obedience, then, would be: the *subjection* of one's judgment and will to a Superior. This subjection, an active exercise on our part, occurs in all matters and at all times. We say, "My will is to do my Superior's will," just as Christ said, "My will is to do the will of Him Who sent Me." However we define it, obedience means that we do what our Superior tells us to do.

Occasionally religious modify this definition of obedience. Quoting Saint Paul, they restrict obedience to "a reasonable service." They use this phrase as a scale on which to weigh a Superior's orders. If an order seems to them meet and just, they obey it; if it seems to them imprudent or unfair, they ignore it. I wonder about this interpretation of obedience. When we vowed obedience, did we vow only "a reasonable service"? And did we reserve to ourselves, as to a Supreme Court of one, the right to decide what commands of our Superiors are or are not "reasonable"? We vowed obedience in all things except sin. We vowed the total submission of our judgment and will to the judgment and will of our Superiors, within the framework of our Rule. "Ours is not to reason why"—that is for our Superiors to do. Besides, a study of the context of Saint Paul's "reasonable service" (Rom. 12:1) shows that this phrase refers not at all to obedience. Saint Paul is urging the Romans to mortify their bodies, to dedicate their bodies to God's service as revelation and reason dictate. That is the meaning of Saint Paul's "reasonable service," or, as recent translations term it, "spiritual service." It would, it seems to me, be far more plausible to associate this phrase with religious chastity than with religious obedience, with which it has no conceivable connection.

Now, your very acceptance of Superiorship was an act of obedience. You accepted it simply because God willed it. And you accepted it with good grace; not like a pastor appointed against his will to a parish, whose first sermon to the people of that parish went something like this: "The Bishop sent me here. I certainly didn't want to come. I loved it where I was, and I don't mind telling you I detest this town of yours." Not exactly the way to win friends and influence people, was it? Nor the way to teach obedience to authority, including his own.

Like your subjects, you, of course, reverence your Rule. For it is the Gospel in shorthand. It contains the Gospel precepts and counsels, and prescribes the means for their observance. Hence it is replete with divine wisdom. Think of it as your road-map to heaven. Then there are your Constitutions—your Baedeker supplementing your road-map. They derive from your Rule, amplify it, apply it detailedly to concrete circumstances. As you know, they do not in themselves bind under penalty of sin; but contempt for them invariably begets contempt for the Rule. You ought to regard them as highly as did a Sister of whom Monsignor Charles H. Doyle tells this story: Sister, a German immigrant, was among a group of immigrants applying for U.S. citizenship papers one day. The judge asked her, "Sister, do you ever read the Constitution?"

"O yah, Judge," she answered, "I read our Constitution every week."

The judge beamed approval. "I hope the rest of you," he told the group, "will imitate Sister. And I hope you will share her fine patriotism, which prompts her to call it 'our' Constitution even before she is a citizen!"

Has it ever struck you how wondrously your Rule and Constitutions simplify the spiritual life? Suppose that you had to experiment, to draw up your own rule of religious life. In what terms would you define religious perfection? Maybe you would make the mistake of the three blind men who came against their first elephant.

"An elephant is a fire-hose," said the first, feeling the elephant's trunk.

"Nonsense!" said the second, feeling the elephant's side; "an elephant is a wall!"

"You're both wrong," said the third, feeling the elephant's tail; "an elephant is a rope!"

In like manner you might define a part of perfection for the whole, or accentuate the negative, or eliminate the positive, or overstress this and understress that, which is the way of heresies. Well, your Rule and Constitutions solve your problem. You have but to follow them.

Sometimes priests meet people who assure them: "I'm a good Catholic, Father. Oh, I don't go to Sunday Mass, but I do provide well for my aged parents." "Good Catholic"? Might not a good Mohammedan do as much? Or: "I'm a good Catholic, Father. It's true, I'm married to a divorcee, but I never eat meat on Friday." "Good Catholic"? Did Christ, Who founded Catholicism, have nothing to say against the remarriage of the divorced? Such people, you see, are trying to define Catholicism in their own terms. They remind us of cafeteria patrons, moving along the counter with their trays, judiciously selecting from the outlay of food the dishes they like, and leaving those they don't like.

Sometimes Superiors choose items of obedience in that fashion. "I'm a good Superior," says one. "Oh, I don't bother with the prescribed silence (after all, we're not Trappists), but I do insist on all the prescribed chapel prayers." Or: "I'm a good Superior. I don't insist on all those chapel prayers (after all, we're not Perpetual Adoration Sisters), but I do insist on the exact fulfillment of all assigned work." Yes, but doesn't Scripture clearly say that "whosoever shall keep the whole law, but offend in one point, is become guilty of all" (James 2:10)? All the precepts of the law, you see, are to be considered as one total and entire law, as a chain of precepts; so that to break one link is to break the whole chain. You must try, rather, to keep the whole chain intact, by obeying in all matters.

I reminded you previously that the authority delegated to you by your Major Superior is limited. Watch that you don't exceed its limits; that you apply to your Major Superior for permissions she has reserved to herself. But don't bother her with trivia—like the nun who, when a priest had said to her, "A lovely day, isn't it, Sister?" answered, "I'll have to go and ask Reverend Mother." It is presumed that you *do* have some authority—that you are not just a pasteboard Superior. That authority should be clearly defined by your Constitutions or your Book of Customs. I trust I am not uncharitable in surmising that the womanly genius for detail might occasionally assert itself in a Major Superior who reserves to herself all kinds of petty exercises of authority, even to ordering the number of lentils to be put in the soup! Self-immersed authority, though, doesn't make for good government. Male religious Superiors usually follow the Roman plan of ruling by delegation ("Divide et impera"). If a male local Superior consulted his Major Superior about trifles, the answer would probably be: "Take care of it yourself. That's why you're a Superior."

It's for you, naturally, to see that any directives from your Major Superior are carried out. What if one of them is so harsh, so patently unjust, as to create a general furore among your Sisters? First, you yourself must pass no unfavorable comment on the directive. Second, you may quietly and respectfully report to the Major Superior the general dissatisfaction with the directive and the reasons for that dissatisfaction. If the Major Superior, deaf to all the dictates of prudence, still insists on the directive, then you say, "Fiat," and by the example of your own obedience you pour oil on the troubled waters in your community. Such obedience makes you touch hands with Christ, Who "became obedient for us, even unto death."

It's part of your obedience, too, to welcome cordially any subject sent to you. She comes in obedience, and you accept her in obedience, without prejudices or prepossessions. Finally, it's part of your obedience that, when your term of office is over, you return to the ranks gracefully, glad to take orders after having given them. If I know you at all, you'll do that: you'll be singing a jubilant *Te Deum* when that day comes for you to move "from the chair to the floor."

Your affectionate uncle,

FATHER C.

14. *"Being Rich, He Became Poor"*

DEAR SISTER,

Thanks for sending for my bi-focal perusal those four articles on religious poverty in the modern world. Since they appeared in a periodical for nuns, I, unveiled and unguimped, had not seen them. I can understand, all right, why you and your Sisters found them frustrating. For one thing, the writing or maybe the translation is so awkward and involved you almost have to hold it upside down to figure out its meaning. For another, the articles are much more articulate in asking the questions about poverty than in giving the answers. Count me, too, among the frustrated.

Surely, religious poverty in the modern world does pose problems. On the one hand, our vowed goal is to imitate the poverty of Christ. His norms of poverty must be ours. "I have given you," He said, "an example: that as I have done . . . , so do you also" (John 13:15). On the other hand, for us to imitate His poverty in all its literal and historical details is neither feasible nor necessary. The changed times, changed social conditions, changed material standards of living impose changed practices. If our poverty is not to be a fettering anachronism, we must in many ways adjust it to the world and the times in which we live—in many ways, but not all ways.

To try to clarify the issue, let's recall what the Gospel tells us about the poverty of Christ. First, His poverty was, of course, voluntary. Saint Paul stresses that point: "Being rich, he became poor, for your sakes; that through his poverty you might be rich" (II Cor. 8:9).

Second, the poverty of Christ, freely chosen, was a real poverty, with nothing fictitious about it. He chose for His birthplace a bleak hillside cave, a shelter for animals. He chose for His first crib a crude manger, a trough for feeding animals. He chose a poor maiden for His mother, a poor carpenter for His foster father. He chose to live for thirty years in a poor cottage in a poor village. During the last three years of His life, when "He went about doing good," He had "not where to lay his head" (Luke 9:58). He made the renunciation of possessions the first test of His disciples: "Go, sell what thou hast, and give to the poor" (Matt. 19:21). Sending His disciples on missionary tours, He commanded that "they should not take anything for the way, but a staff only: no scrip, no bread, nor money in their purse" (Mark 6:8). Finally, in death as in life, He still had "not where to lay his head": He was buried in another man's tomb.

Third, the poverty of Christ was a poverty of daily wants, privations, hardships. But it was not the poverty of famishment (His physique had to be sturdy to endure His forty-day fast on the mountain, the incessant travels and labors of His public ministry); not the poverty of the squalid shack (Mary's refined instincts undoubtedly abhorred filth); not the poverty of rags (even the sophisticated Roman soldiers thought His cloak worth casting lots for). His was a clean and respectable poverty that consisted in the simple use of the simple necessities of life, the avoidance of all superfluities and comforts and luxuries, the complete detachment from all things material, the complete contentment with His lowly lot at all times. It was poverty both in fact and in spirit.

Now, I said that for us to copy this poverty of Christ in all its literal and historical details is neither feasible nor necessary. As individual religious, we must, indeed, renounce worldly possessions: renounce the ownership of them, by a solemn vow of poverty; or renounce the use, administration, benefits of them, by a simple vow. But must we have nowhere to lay our heads? Whereas the mission of Christ and the Apostles was itinerant, ours is for the most part stationary: we must have residences—and the Church so decrees. Our residences are to be, surely, the residences of poor people, plain and unpretentious as was the Holy House of Nazareth. But they need not duplicate the Holy House in architecture. (Like the houses in Nazareth today, that House was probably a one-story, flat-roofed, box-like structure of stone or of baked mud.) Nor need our residences duplicate the Holy House in appointments. (In a tropical country, it lacked heat. Its floors were probably of packed dirt. It was lighted by candles or by oil-lamps suspended from rafters. Its water was carried in jars from the village well. Its stove was a crude construction of stone sides and an iron grill.) Without prejudice to poverty, we are certainly allowed to have in our residences modern heating and lighting, modern plumbing, modern kitchen and laundry equipment, modern furniture, modern household appliances. Our poverty doesn't demand that, in these respects, we turn the clock back twenty centuries.

And what of our travels? Christ and the Apostles travelled by foot over a territory approximately thirty miles wide and a hundred miles long. They took with them neither food nor money. (The common "purse" that Judas carried was used only, Saint John implies, for alms-giving and buying the items prescribed for the Paschal supper.) They ate what they could find or what friends gave them. They slept in houses, gardens, or under wayside hedges. But we? We must travel by car or bus or railroad or airplane often hundreds of miles and sometimes even thousands. And for our travels we simply must carry money in our purse for fare, food, and perhaps lodging at our destination.

How then, can we religious imitate the poverty of Christ

today? We can and must imitate His poverty in spirit. Here, indeed, "the letter killeth, but the spirit quickeneth" (II Cor. 3:6). Like Christ, we must restrict ourselves to the use of the necessary; must remain detached from the things we use; must gladly accept whatever privations and inconveniences the common life entails; must be content "with having food, and wherewith to be covered" (I Tim. 6:8). Apart from all the adjustments and compromises that time and place have necessitated, our standards of poverty must still be those of Him Who "being rich, became poor."

In practice, our poverty may be defined, I think, as the obtaining of permission to use what is necessary. This definition applies to every one of us: to Superiors, who are merely the custodians (not the owners) of the common funds; to subjects long in the community as well as the newly-professed. It applies to us whether we're at home or abroad. Till our dying day, our poverty humbly asks, like a little child, "May I? May I use this? May I buy that? May I accept this gift? May I give that gift away?" It's a curtailment, you see, not only of our goods, but of our liberty. Thus it's really obedience under another name.

Naturally, as Superior you give yourself permission to use what you need (and only what you need). You ask yourself, "May I?" and you answer, "You may"—and that's no painful procedure. But remember that for many of your subjects, especially the old ones, the words "May I?" are among the most awkward words in human speech; so awkward that, rather than speak them, some bashful subjects prefer to lack necessities. Let your kindness, then, ease and encourage the requests of your Sisters, persuading them that you do indeed count it "more blessed to give than to receive." Let your answer customarily be a hearty "You may," with trust in the good sense and honesty of the petitioners. If in a rare case you feel obliged to answer, "You may not," explain the reason for your refusal; so that, though Sister goes away empty-handed, she will not go away heavy-hearted.

There used to be somewhere an octogenarian Superior who met all his subjects' requests for toothpaste by mumbling, "Nonsense! Use some salt!" He himself, you see, was totally toothless. Maybe he loved not poverty so much as money. Maybe his concern was to advance not so much the perfection of his subjects as his own rating with his Superior General. ("See what an excellent financial report Brother Dodo has sent in!") Whatever his motives, he forced his subjects to periodical violations of poverty; to accumulate their own money and purchase their own toothpaste. (Incidentally, you'll save time and trouble all around if you keep the ordinary toilet articles in a hall cupboard, with the understanding that the Sisters are to take them as they need them.) In every way, it's safer and saner to overabound with permissions than to stint.

Through carelessness, Superiors can violate poverty by running over the margin in one of two ways: by stinginess—avarice under a gentler name; or by extravagance. Behold the stingy Superior—Sister Avaritia. She practically starves her subjects ("People eat too much!"); freezes them ("Winter does not officially start till December twenty-first!"); blinds them ("Tests show a 50-watt ceiling bulb is adequate lighting in a room!"); makes them patch their habits till they are all patches and no habits ("They that wear soft garments are in the houses of kings!"). She dotes on second-hand purchases. She rarely gives permission for purchases of new things, and always with a look of acute pain. She sends all her sick Sisters to a chiropractor who manipulates their spines gratis. She urges her Sisters to write home for money for their needs. If a Sister must travel, she doles out the exact fare, not a dime beyond it. That's Sister Avaritia. In the world she'd have been known as Madame Scrooge.

Now behold her opposite—Sister Extravagantia. She

places in the community room a petty-cash box with a sign, "Permission granted—Help yourself." Her Sisters, requesting permissions for major items, have hardly opened their mouths when she says, "Get anything you want." She insists that they spend all gifts of money on themselves—to "brighten up" their rooms and their lives. She questions the cook if left-overs are served. She spends small fortunes on private whims: installing or walling up doors, changing draperies and furniture, redecorating a chapel that her predecessor decorated. Never having earned a dollar in her pre-convent days, she has not the dimmest notion of the value of a dollar. Her financial records—those, that is, that she keeps—are a jumble, full of mysterious "miscellaneous" entries. Heaven help her successor!

Now, I hardly need tell you that, in matters of poverty, you should veer neither to the left with Avaritia, nor to the right with Extravagantia: you should keep to the middle of the road. You should, I mean, limit your expenditures of convent funds to what's necessary for the decent upkeep of the convent, and your permissions to your Sisters to the use of what's necessary for their health and work and legitimate recreation. The convent necessities depend, of course, on the age and the condition of the convent. The Sisters' necessities? They likewise depend on the state of a Sister's health and on the type of work assigned to her. The term "necessity" has to be somewhat elastic.

Some things all religious do need. First and foremost, all need adequate food. In old catalogues of Catholic boarding schools, you frequently see the assuring phrase, "Good, substantial food." That phrase, I can testify from my own youthful experiences, often covered a multitude of sins, both dietetic and culinary. But the idea behind the phrase was sound: the idea that students, presumably moilers and toilers, needed good fare. So, surely, do your hard-working Sisters. Feed them well. Start their day with a "good, substantial" breakfast—of more than toast and coffee, and with ample time to eat it. See that, after the morning's ordeal in school, they have a "good, substantial" lunch—of more than peanut butter sandwiches and milk. Let them have free access to the convent pantry after school with no cupboards padlocked. Provide for them a "good, substantial" supper—of more than wieners, beans, and apples. There is no poverty in ruining their stomachs with inadequate and inedible food, and then paying enormous hospital bills for their happy recovery. I am not advocating, you understand, any Louis XIV cuisine, but merely the "good, substantial" food your Sisters need to keep well, pray well, and work well.

Besides food, your Sisters need clothing, which should be and invariably is decent. They need equipment, such as, perhaps, books or typewriters, for the special work assigned them. They need proper medical care in sickness. They need recreation. The good Saint Francis de Sales terms it a fault not to take recreation oneself nor to allow others to take it. Why a fault? Because we need recreation scarcely less than we need sleep. We need it to relax tensions, to purge emotions, to refresh weary faculties, to foster community spirit. You should normally insist, then, that all your Sisters take part in the recreation. It is, after all, a community exercise.

Admittedly, many Sisters find the recreation period the lowest ebb of the day. For them, it is not the pause that refreshes, but the pause that depresses. And why? It may be that recreation in their community isn't recreation at all. Like an inquiring reporter, I have asked at a number of convents, "What do you do at recreation?" One answer, in the Deep South, went: "We sit on the veranda and rock and talk and fight mosquitoes, and crunch horehound candy the Superior passes around." Another answer: "We walk in two's around the convent garden path, or around the portico if it's raining, and discuss a spiritual topic the Superior has assigned us." A third answer: "We sit on straight-back chairs around the table in the community room discoursing silly nothings." A fourth: "We watch the NBC news telecast the first half-hour, the CBS news telecast the second half-hour." If recreation means any of these drab goings-on, small wonder, say I, that it bores some religious to tears.

What, actually, does recreation mean? Webster answers: "A refreshment of strength and spirits after toil; diversion or a mode of diversion; play." It lies essentially in a change of activity, not in a withdrawal into a vacuum. A *sine qua non* of it is relaxation, not regimentation. Some Sisters, the older ones, may like to sit and do needle-work and engage in pleasant conversation. Some, the middle-aged, may like to play bridge or canasta or chess or checkers. Some, the young, may like to cluster around the piano and sing about smiling Irish eyes or a daring young man on a flying trapeze or old man MacDonald's farm. It is of the essence that they all do what they enjoy doing, and thus find Webster's "refreshment of strength and spirits" in doing it. So, dear Sister, let them.

Your affectionate uncle,

FATHER C.

15. *"With These We are Content"*

DEAR SISTER,

You might call this letter "Paralipomenon," meaning "things left over" or "things left out." In it, that is, you'll find a few stray thoughts on poverty that the clock didn't permit me to include in my previous letter on that vow. No apocalyptic penetrations, you may be sure, but just pedestrian observations.

To begin with, the poverty vowed by different religious communities differs in degrees, according to the Rule and Constitutions of each community. Yet the over-all aim, the grand-scale ideal, of the poverty of all communities is identical: the loving imitation of the poverty of Christ. The good religious of all communities, therefore, ever strive to approach that ideal. They realize that the "letter"—the measured observance of poverty only to an extent strictly prescribed—"killeth"; but the "spirit"—the generous observance of poverty to lengths unprescribed—"quickeneth." They ask not, "How far can I go?"—that is, without violating poverty; they ask, rather, "How close can I come?"—that is, to the poverty of Christ Himself.

I suggested, you'll recall, this as a working definition of poverty: the obtaining of permission to use what's necessary. A luxury is not a necessity; and people might well be perplexed if a convent, the home of professedly poor religious, were the most imposing house in its area, the best equipped with modern appliances, the most richly furnished. A comment of Saint Francis de Sales would here be in point: "To desire to be poor but not inconvenienced by poverty, is to desire the honor of poverty and the convenience of riches." Such "poverty" would be a mere state of mind.

Yet our poverty need not mean destitution. Some newly professed young religious, you know, expect it to mean nothing short of that. In their novitiate, they probably gorged themselves on stories about Saint Anthony of Egypt, who shuffled about the desert clad in sackcloth and chewing on weeds; or about Saint Simon Stylites, who sat naked atop his column, baking in the Egyptian sun; or about Saint Simon Stock, who slept inside a hollow oak in an English forest; or about Saint Francis of Assisi and his first followers, who lived in wattle huts along the Rivo Torto. Then, after profession, when they arrive at their first appointment, they critically survey their surroundings. "Poverty," they muse, "means want. Here I live in a fine house, eat fine meals, have all the clothing I need, receive excellent medical care when I'm sick. Where's my want?" Our poverty today is, admittedly, not quite the state of being in want. And if it isn't that, it's because a wise Church has so decreed, in view of our given apostolates of preaching, teaching, nursing, and the rest. Those apostolates would suffer if, in our fulfillment of them, we were perpetually harassed by worries about out next lump of coal, our next crust of bread, our next pair of shoes, our next bar of soap, our next pen and pencil, our next dollar for necessary travels. We'd have time to do little else but worry about temporalities.

One writer makes the point that, though not in want ourselves, we religious should remember that some of the laymen we deal with are. So, he urges, let there be no pressure on school children to contribute to campaigns ("Remember, children, our room must lead!") or to sell raffle tickets or to get costumes for plays or special clothes for processions. Undoubtedly, such pressures can inflict real hardships on some poor parents, especially those of large families. A practical point, I think, well worth the remembering.

Your Rule and Constitutions set the norms of your poverty. The approved customs of your community throw further light on those norms. Those customs arose to meet the demands of circumstances. They're approved because they're sane and sound. Sometimes, though, communities develop customs diametrically opposed to poverty. I can think of no more flagrant example than one narrated by Thomas Walsh in his life of Saint Teresa of Avila. Some male religious of the sixteenth century, he relates, had so relaxed their poverty that, without any official disapproval, they individually acquired lands, money, benefices. They adorned their habits with bright brass buttons, and ruffles, and colored cords and tassels. Some had jars of rose water in their cells. Some collected musical instruments such as organs, harpsichords, or even such profane and proscribed devices as lyres and barbitons. It took a Visitor General from Rome, armed with papal decrees and scissors and a huge wastebasket, to restore them to some semblance of poor men.

Modern parallels, involving perhaps no buttons or barbitons but involving the same exercise of ownership, are not altogether lacking. Somewhere in the land, I am reliably informed, there is a monastery in which every religious is represented by a cigar box in a hall cupboard with the owner's name neatly printed on his box. Though in solemn vows, each religious puts into his box whatever returns his friendship with Mammon intermittently nets him. Whenever he wants to buy anything or to go anywhere, he simply, with no permission required, withdraws the desired funds from his box, and goes on his way humming. A custom? Yes. An approved custom? I'm quite sure that the sainted founder of that Order would not approve of it at all; that if on leave from heaven he visited that monastery, with a holy snort he would toss those cigar boxes, and maybe their owners, out the nearest window. For he was avowedly the foe of piggy-banks.

More common, you know, is the private or secret cigar box (or its equivalent in feminine circles) kept in one's room. The funds in it, accumulated from unreturned change and unreported donations, serve as a security against refused permissions—the sort of insurance policy held by Ananias and Saphira. A custom? Certainly. But an approved custom? It's a custom that, involving the unwarranted possession and the independent use of money, knocks poverty into a cocked hat. It calls for decisive repression.

No doubt about it, the good old U. S. A. poses a constant threat to our religious poverty. Americans are so generous, and often so well-circumstanced, that, if they like us at all, they can't shake our hands without slipping greenbacks to us. I've seen, mind you, religious come to our shores from lands where, in the strictest observance of poverty, they had literally never touched coins. But big-hearted Americans poured coins into the hands of those religious. The religious jingled them, smiled, exclaimed, "Is nice!"—and went on spending sprees that astounded us natives. Just see what happens to us at Christmas! "The kings of Tharsis and the isles"—complete strangers—"bring gifts." And what stacks of mail come to us, much of it with fives and tens enclosed, with the underlined insistence. "This is for *you,* not for the community!" I tell you, dear Sister, we ought to fear Americans bearing gifts. We ought to fear that, when they pile those gifts into our arms, they will make us lose our greatest treasure of all—our religious poverty.

The mention of gifts may raise a question in your mind: What should you, as Superior, do about the gifts your Sisters receive? If the gifts are clothing, books, desk equipment, religious articles or anything else that would help a Sister in her religious life and work, give her glad permission to accept and use them. If the gifts are superfluities—the latest, for example, in health gadgets or toilet luxuries for milady—gently urge Sister to unload them on relatives and friends who set high store on such things. If the gifts are money? A rule of your Institute ought to state clearly that all gifts of money accrue not to the receivers, but to the Institute. Otherwise you'll develop an odious caste system of have's and have-not's, with the have-not's envying the have's. It's much safer and fairer if all money gifts go into the common coffers towards the common needs.

In the interest of poverty, of course, we are to conserve carefully the things committed to our use. We are not to ruin a good habit by gardening or painting in it—or to ruin books by tossing them about—or to ruin furniture by leaving windows open in rainstorms—or to neglect the proper care of the convent car—or to burn down the convent by letting a hot iron stand on a wooden table. Yet, we are *not* to make a fetish of poverty by pushing it to absurd extremes. If we do so, our poverty, instead of freeing us from worldly cares and distractions, becomes in itself an all-absorbing care and distraction.

"I wasted water," a scrupulous observant of poverty may confess. But when does the use of water become the waste of water? Must we, in our concern for poverty, measure out water with an eye-dropper? When Christ told the servants at Cana to fill the vessels with water, He certainly didn't add, "But don't spill any!" "I wasted soap," another punctilious religious confesses. Again, at what point does the use of soap become the waste of soap? How many bubbles, strictly, make a bath? Mary Magdalen, laving the feet of Christ with ointment, was evidently lavish in the use of it, for "the house was filled with the odor of the ointment" (John 12:3). Yet Christ didn't say, "You are using more, Mary, than is really necessary!"

In the interest of poverty, we are to conserve and take proper care of the material things in our lives. But in the conservation and care of them we are *not* to act like misers:

hoarding scraps of paper and bits of string, mopping plates clean with bread after meals, flicking off lights the precise second we can grope through corridors without them, wearing shoes through to the ground, writing with pencils that are one-inch stubs, filling letter-paper from top to bottom and side to side, praying from books worn illegible through use, and so on, and so on. After miraculously multiplying the five barley loaves and the two fishes to feed five thousand, Our Lord did, indeed, tell the Apostles, "Gather up the fragments that remain, lest they be lost" (John 6:12). But note, first, the largesse of His miracle: He provided for the crowd twelve baskets more of food than they actually needed. Note, second, that the unused food was worth gathering up: it was, to state it bluntly, not garbage. Can't you imagine that what Our Lord told the Apostles is what, say, any priest might tell his altar boys at the end of a day's outing (if any fragments were left!): "Gather up the left-over sandwiches, boys. We can give them to the back-door callers at the rectory"? I think it safe to conclude that Christ, by these words, advocated no nervous niggardliness, but sensible thriftiness.

Never forget, dear Sister, that what counts most is poverty in spirit. Without it, as Judas tragically proved, poverty in fact is worthless. And this poverty in spirit expresses itself in two forms: contentment with what we have or haven't, and detachment from what we use. We are truly poor if we can say with the great Saint Paul: "I have learned, in whatsoever state I am, to be content therewith. I know both how to be brought low, and I know how to abound . . . , both to be full and to be hungry; both to abound and to suffer need" (Phil. 4:11,12). Indifference like that means detachment—and detachment means joy.

Your affectionate uncle,

FATHER C.

16. *"The Pure of Heart"*

Dear Sister,

No, I hadn't planned to write a letter on the vow of chastity, because I felt I'd be carrying coals to Newcastle. Sisters everywhere, I mean, have so high and holy a regard for chastity that their Superiors need harbor few misgivings concerning it. But, since you've asked for it ("to complete the triptych of the vows"), I'll oblige you with a few suggestions, nothing more than cautions that act as guardian angels of chastity.

Naturally, in most of its aspects, the religious chastity of subjects lies beyond the supervision of Superiors. It is intensely personal and private. Though it involves the sublimation of an appetite of the body, it originates deep within the soul. The mind and the will are its well-springs, as Our Lord stressed when He beatified "the pure of heart." If the well is clear, the streams that flow from it in words and actions will ever run clear.

You cannot, of course, control the thoughts of your subjects. Yet you can, as Superior, help them in their thought-control by providing them with only the best of reading material. I think it safe to say that most of the external temptations of religious against chastity come from old man Gutenberg's invention, the press. See that in your convent magazine rack you have, in addition to your Catholic publications, only the best of secular magazines, the current-events magazines helpful to your teachers in their work. Don't allow in that rack any of the popular fiction or picture magazines, which frequently contain material sexational enough to raise even blasé eyebrows.

Television programs also need some monitoring. They have not as yet, thank God, gravitated to the depths of most movies today. Few of them are morally objectionable: their besetting sin is vapidity rather than obscenity. But most of them do bring the world smack into the convent: the world with its pagan standards and allurements; the very world that, for the safety of their souls, religious left. And that's why a few years ago Rome, you'll remember, restricted the TV viewing of non-cloistered religious (for cloistered it's entirely taboo) to two kinds of programs—religious programs, and educational programs. Beyond those two, all is a Sahara anyhow.

In addition to magazines and television there are two person-to-person dangers to chastity against which you must try to shield your Sisters. The first is—yes, you guessed it—particular friendship. Now, this term, it seems to me, is somewhat inaccurate. Isn't any and every friendship of necessity "particular"—a friendship for a particular person? I can, as a song says, have "a smile on my face for the whole human race"; for all mankind I can have good will and charity, but hardly friendship. A considerably more precise term here, I think, would be "exclusive" friendship—like a friendship of a teen-age boy and girl who "go steady," cutting themselves off from association with the rest of the teen-age community, living on a planet of their own.

What's wrong with such an exclusive friendship in religious life? Everything. To begin with, it's based not on any spiritual or intellectual or cultural affinity, but on sentimentality or physical attraction or both. Secondly, it's a reprehensible withdrawal from the common life into a closed corporation of two. Thirdly, it's fraught with possibilities of serious moral harm, as all theologians warn. A Superior, therefore, must break up such an exclusive friendship as soon as she detects it. As Father John H. McGoey, S.F.M., explains, "Whenever two nuns are seen holding hands, lavishing endearments on each other, particularly caresses of any kind . . . persistently exclude all others, or neglect their duties to be with each other, or do not respond in charity to the needs of others, there is room for considerable thought." If the friendship persists, the Superior must have one of the twosome transferred elsewhere, and all lines of communication between them severed. The salvation of two souls may well be at stake.

Are we here ruling out *all* friendships in religious life? Absolutely not. Solomon eulogizes a true friend as "a strong defence . . . a treasure . . . the medicine of life and immortality." He exclaims: "Blessed is he that findeth a true friend" (Ecclus. 25:12)—and no footnote adds, "Except in religious life." Without friends, a religious community is but a gallery of faces, smiling perhaps, but remote and impersonal. We inevitably have more in common with some of our convent companions than with others. Perhaps we hailed from the same town, parish, school. Our temperaments, talents, tastes, and interests match remarkably. Especially do we share the same sense of humor, probably the first of all common denominators. We thoroughly relish each other's company and conversation; we mutually profit by them. Nature and grace evidently destined us to be not just associates, but friends. Our friendship, however, does *not* wall us off from the rest of the community. Far from constituting a drawback in our religious life, it is a powerful stimulus for good—and we should thank God for it.

Another person-to-person danger against which you must safeguard your Sisters is called "suspicious intimacy"—intimacy, that is, with any men. Perhaps the old warning, "*Nunquam solus cum sola*" ("Never a man alone with a woman"), overshoots the mark; at least it expresses meager confidence in all members of both sexes. It needs interpretation. Suppose some woman comes to the friary parlor to see me about offering a Mass for her intention. Must she (*"nunquam sola"*) bring her aunt or her grandmother with her, and must I (*"nunquam solus"*) bring another friar with me to witness the simple transaction? Or suppose that before opening a convent retreat I want to discuss some detail of it with the Sister Superior. Must she march the whole community into the parlor to monitor my speech and hers? The big word in this context is "intimacy."

Father Eugene Boylan, O.C.R., with fine insight, states these two pertinent principles (here slightly adapted): 1. Regard as dangerous any *friendship* of a Sister with any man. 2. Regard *with grave suspicion* any such friendship formed *after a Sister's religious profession.* Suspect the latter friendship if not for what it already is, at least for what it may become. And these principles cover, I don't hesitate to say it, any close friendship between a Sister and a priest, no less than between a Sister and a layman. Both Sister's and Father's intentions at the start may be entirely guileless, even entirely good. Sister, for example, may be attracted to Father by his marked piety, counsel, and understanding—all gifts of the Holy Ghost. Or Father, newly ordained, may find in Sister the pleasant companionship and helpful encouragement—both good in themselves—denied him by a harsh, cold rectory life. But when their acquaintance deepens into friendship, when they begin to meet frequently or to hold frequent telephone conversations or to exchange frequent notes or gifts, they are treading a mine-field where any step can trigger off shattering explosions. It is then that you should warn Sister, as a wise old Superior warned one of her charges in a similar case, "Remember, Sister, that he is a man and you are a woman." To reinforce your warning, you might quote the Spanish proverb: "Between a man saint and a woman saint must stand a high wall, if they are to remain saints." Your concern here would be prudence, not prurience.

Purity is, of course, not prudery, the seeing of evil where none exists. You must watch that none of your Sisters confuse the two. Like the Sister who, because a six-year-old girl had come to school wearing a sleeveless dress, sent her home with a note to her mother, "Dress this child chastely!" Or like several Sisters in a girl's academy who, when some of their senior charges went to their first prom at a nearby Catholic boys' academy, anxiously burned vigil-lights as though the girls were walking into the very jaws of death. Sisters ought to realize that the boy-girl attraction is natural; which means it's an attraction authorized by God Himself as a necessary first step towards marriage and the continuance of the race.

See that your Sisters let no prudery obstruct their duty to explain, when teaching the Commandments, what the Sixth and the Ninth Commandments really mean. They *don't* mean "keeping one's armor bright" any more than they mean "keeping one's shoes shined." And the breaking of them doesn't mean merely "doing something bad"—a term that covers the breaking of any of the other eight Commandments as well. The explanation should be given deftly, and many books propose the wording for it; and it should be suited to the age and the mental capacity of the children receiving it. But it *should* be given. So that when a child confesses, "I did something bad," the confessor's inquiry won't reveal that the "something bad" consisted in sticking out a tongue at an elder brother or pulling the hair of a younger sister.

A subject may come to you and express abnormal difficulties with her personal chastity. Perhaps those difficulties are pathological. Perhaps she definitely needs medical care—from a woman doctor if she shrinks from approaching a male doctor. Or perhaps her troubles arise from a woeful ignorance of the facts of life. As a girl she may have grown up in a hot-house academy, a lily-laden atmosphere where the word "sex" was unknown. From there she may have moved into an air-tight novitiate, and from there into an almost air-tight convent. Along the line, puzzled by physiological developments within her, she may have asked a Superior for needful information, and may have got the answer, "Sister, you have a dirty mind!" (It has happened!) So she has gone on her way confused, frightened, tortured, imagining everything connected with sex as sinful. Such a poor soul needs light. Give it to her yourself or through a good book on the subject. Here, ignorance is by no means bliss.

Most women have a natural instinct for cleanliness. Well, an old clerical saying calls Sisters "women twice over." And that they are. Their homes are twice as immaculate as other women's, their linens twice as white, their handwriting twice as neat. And their hearts twice as pure. So long as they go on loving Our Lord and Our Lady the way they do, you need worry little about them.

Your affectionate uncle,

Father C.

17. *"They Murmured"*

Dear Sister,

I can't resist the temptation to chortle, "I told you so!" I told you that, try as you might, you would never be able to please all your subjects. The instance you relate drolly proves the point. You tried to gilt-edge young Sister Anonyma's feastday last Saturday with a "Waldorf-Astoria" dinner of turkey and all the trimmings, and Sister thanked you effusively. Yet when cold cuts and potato chips were served for supper, you overheard Sister darkly accusing you of "stinginess," though the supper menu was entirely the idea of the tired Sister cook. (It's odd, considering how intensely spiritual we religious are, how much ado we can make about food!) An unfair criticism? Of course it was. But then such criticisms are the inheritance and the cup of Superiors. They are—and they always have been.

Monsignor Knox somewhere points out the broken-record repetition of the sentence, "They murmured," in the Book of Exodus. "They," of course, were the Chosen People en route from Egypt to the Promised Land. God Himself had designated their leaders, Moses and Aaron. He had wrought ten first-class miracles to free them from their slavery to Pharaoh. He had parted the waters of the Red Sea to let them pass through dry-shod, and had made those waters engulf the army that Pharaoh had sent in pursuit of them. He had given them a special cloud to direct them by day and a pillar of fire to shield them by night. He had fed them manna and quail and had made fountains gush from rocks to quench their thirst. Yet "they murmured." Like spoiled children, they murmured at every new inconvenience their desert journey entailed. They dared not murmur against God Himself. Instead, they murmured against His appointees, Moses and Aaron. Eventually Moses upbraided them: "Who are we? Your murmuring is not against us, but against the Lord" (Exod. 16:8).

Well, God's Chosen People, His religious, still murmur. That they do so gives pause for thought. Hasn't their vocation freed them from the bondage of the world? Hasn't it brought them into the blessed freedom and spaciousness of the desert? Don't they have Manna from heaven for their daily food, and gushing fountains of grace on all sides of them? Are they not led by divinely appointed guides? Yet they murmur. Maybe, suggests Monsignor Knox, the desert is to blame. Maybe their isolation from the general populace and its crowded activities and distractions forces them to watch one another and especially their Superiors—too closely. They watch, and they talk.

Like the Israelites, they blame the Superiors for everything that goes amiss, everything that inconveniences them. Does the roof leak or the furnace fail? Why, they demand, didn't she (you) have them checked last summer (when you weren't yet Superior)? Is there a mouse in the convent? Why doesn't she (you) contract with those exterminator people to service the place monthly (when they don't bother to set the mouse-traps you've bought)? Does a Sister have a nervous breakdown? Why couldn't she (you) have seen it coming on and have prevented it (when from the outset you urged Sister, in vain, to consult a neurologist)? Are the schoolrooms overcrowded? Why didn't she (you) limit the registration (when you tried to, but the pastor kept carolling to his flock, "O come, *all* ye faithful")? O yes, the critics, like the poor, you'll have ever with you. Their criticism may considerably retard their own advancement towards perfection, but it can considerably hasten yours. It can, that is, if you learn to say with King David: "It is good for me that thou hast humbled me. . . ." (Ps. 118:71).

In a way, your role as Superior was prefigured in the Old Testament. On the annual solemn Day of Atonement, you'll recall, the Israelites led a ram to the High Priest. It wasn't an anti-social ram, a public-enemy ram, addicted to butting little children and old people or chewing up clothes on washlines. It was an ordinary, well-meaning, well-mannered, friendly sort of ram that harmed nobody. Yet the High Priest pressed his hands firmly on its head, and, while the ram must have blinked and wondered what was going on, he chanted loudly, calling down on that head the iniquities of all the Israelities. Then the High Priest either coaxed the unsuspecting ram to the edge of a cliff and shoved it off into space, or he shooed it off into the desert to waste away of malnutrition. That ram is you, Sister. Upon your harmless head descend all the grievances of your community, as though you were responsible for them. And though you're not ultimately shoved off a cliff, you *are* turned to pasture in a desert, isolated in your authority. Well, if the Chosen People feel relieved after loading their grievances upon you, you've rendered them a therapeutic service.

A few religious, I suspect, were born critics. They are sprung from the loins of Ismael of old, of whom it was prophesied: "He shall be a wild man: his hand will be against all men, . . . and he shall pitch his tents over against the tents of all his brethren" (Gen. 16:12). Such a one, evidently, was a Sister in one of Monsignor Doyle's stories, who told him that, no, she had not attended the funeral of her Mother Provincial, but was "cordially in favor of it." And such a one was the Brother who, after brushes with a dozen Superiors in a dozen houses, reported at his thirteenth house, bent his knee to the Superior there, and said in one breath: "Your blessing, Father. I hear you don't treat your subjects very well." During their novitiate, these born critics prudently kept mum, prudently kept their Ismael's hand up their sleeve and their Ismael's tents unpitched. But ever since then, they have waged open war, hot or cold, against the powers that be. In their book, all Superiors are morons or fanatics or frauds. The highest encomium they ever accord to any Superior is, "Well, I've seen a worse one, though I can't remember where."

What made them such chronic critics? In their infancy, perhaps their parents took matches and scissors away from them. Perhaps in kindergarten a teacher slapped them for throwing sand at other children. Perhaps in grade school a janitor shouted at them for sailing paper airplanes out of windows. Perhaps in high school a chemistry teacher failed them for blowing up a laboratory. Only a psychiatrist, through long and patient couch-side inquisition, could discover the deep origins of their maladjustment, their antipathy for authority. Or it could be that the root of all their hostility to Superiors is nothing but plain envy. At all events, you cannot change them. You can only pray for them, and bear with their constant carping.

I am sure, though, that the majority of religious who criticize Superiors do so not out of ingrained disrespect, but out of ignorance or misunderstanding. A Sister, for instance, who taught art in a high school noted the arrival of a large box of social study maps, ordered by her Superior and Principal who also happened to teach social studies. "Look at that!" the Sister exclaimed to another Sister. "Hundreds and hundreds of dollars' worth of maps, and I can't get even three easels I need!" What the art teacher did not know, however, was that the Superintendent of Schools, after an inspection, had ordered the Principal to get those maps.

Suppose you've been summoned to a week-end meeting at the motherhouse. You may, if you want, "fold your tent like the Arabs and silently steal away." Some Superiors would. At home, they're as secretive as the Sphynx, disclosing to the community not even such information of common interest as the name of the newly appointed convent confessor. Going abroad, they move in a cloud of mystery, like cuttle-fish, and not even their Assistant Superiors know whither or why. True, your subjects have no right to know where you are going, nor have you any duty to tell them. But why not tell them, to forestall the uncharitable conjectures of some, and to allay the idle curiosity of most? "Let there be light." Let them ordinarily know what you're doing or plan to do, and why. I can't guarantee that your candor will disarm all criticism, but it will reduce it appreciably.

In another letter on another topic, I quoted Cowper's mighty line, "Our discontent is from comparison." Comparison, I dare say, is the basis also of most criticism. I can't forget hearing, for example, two elderly ladies on a Buffalo bus one day discussing the new Buffalo weatherman. The one spoke approvingly of him. The other said: "I don't know why you like *him*. Why, the man before him, that Barney Wiggins, used to give us much nicer weather!" In much the same way, you can be sure, your subjects compare you to your predecessor: "Why are we getting up on Holy Saturday at 7:00? Sister Gate of Heaven always let us sleep till 7:30." Or they compare you to Superiors in other houses of your Institute: "I hear Sister Mystic Rose gives her community bacon for breakfast not just once a week, the way Sister Clare does to us, but three times." You must accept such comparisons, always odious and often fatuous, as the nuisance tax on the honors of Superiorship.

How should you react to your critics—to those who criticize you to your face, and to those who criticize you behind your back? First of all, there is no sense in rushing to your room, locking the door, and bursting into tears. If that's your penchant, you'd better have a gross of Kleenex on hand. Instead, slip quietly into the chapel and examine your conscience, to discover honestly whether you have or haven't deserved the criticism. If you have deserved it, thank Our Lord for it, and resolve to remove the reason for it. Remember, your critic has rendered you a priceless service. As Goethe says, she has shown you not what you can do, but what you should do. If, however, you're certain you haven't deserved the criticism, ask Our Lord to help you immediately to forgive and forget it, to bear the critic no ill will, to continue your motherly interest in her. By Our Lord's word and example, you have no other choice.

Once in a while the criticism is so childish, so picayune, that the best treatment of it is to ignore it altogether. Maybe you've heard the story about the college tower-clock. The campus residents complained to the care-taker that the clock ran slow. The towns-people complained to him that the clock ran fast. He listened, with much nodding of the head, to each group, and assured each, "I will certainly take care of that." Then he did nothing about it and everybody was satisfied. His solution was also that of a wise old Superior General I used to know. When a local Superior came to him and complained about the irrationality of a subject, the General said: "Yes, he is a very peculiar man. I shall see what can be done about him." When that same subject came to him and complained about the irrationality of that same local Superior, the General said: "Yes, he is a very peculiar man. I shall see what can be done about him." And since nothing actually could be done, the General did nothing; and the two peculiar men continued their peculiar ways, with no great harm done.

Well, dear Sister, the Chosen People in the desert go on murmuring. When their murmuring is against you, try to bear it in patience, the virtue to which Saint Bonaventure attributes the sainthood of so many religious Superiors.

Accept the murmuring maybe in reparation for maybe a mite of murmuring that maybe you yourself might have done against a Moses or an Aaron maybe somewhere along the line in a former existence. Maybe?

Your affectionate uncle,

FATHER C.

18. "*Dispensers of His Mysteries*"

DEAR SISTER,

This letter will talk about the men in your life. Don't be startled: I mean us priests, the men who are your chaplains, pastors, confessors, spiritual directors, retreat masters. It's as important, I think, that you understand us as that we understand you.

As a diminutive altar boy, I used to gaze at priests with grave wonder. I regarded them as some mysterious race apart, especially my parish priests—Capuchins with sandalled bare feet and brown robes, and (most of them) patriarchal beards. Vaguely, I associated them with the long-robed figures in our stained-glass church windows, with the long-robed statues in the niches above our altars. I never thought of them as having had fathers and mothers, as having come from homes. I supposed they had been born priests, old ones at that. I knew that inside their ancient, fortress-like monastery they chanted prayers: for I had heard them through open chapel windows. But did they ever eat or sleep or wash hands and faces or get colds or headaches or stomach-aches? I wasn't sure.

All I knew for sure was that in surplice and stole they baptized little babies who always cried; that they sat in dark confessionals where people whispered to them and they whispered back; that they hurried from their monastery to some Catholic home where someone was said to be dying; that they sprinkled holy water on coffins surrounded by six tall candles; that they traced little crosses in the air over new Rosaries people brought to them in the sacristy; that they read things out of a book to nervous brides and grooms at weddings; that from the pulpit on Sundays they called people "Dearly Beloved" and talked to them about going to heaven; that in heavy gold or white or purple or green or red vestments, like those of the Three Kings, they moved solemnly about the altar speaking Latin, sometimes in a cloud of incense; that on Mondays, Wednesdays, and Fridays, to a chorused greeting of "Good *morn*-ing, *Fa*-ther," they entered classrooms and asked children who made them and why and such things. That's all I knew about them. They were, I was sure, as totally different from other people as their gold chalices were from other people's china cups.

Well, as a priest myself I now know that, in some ways, my youthful concept of priests was correct. We *are* a strange race apart, as were the Levites of old. We *are*, in the sense that Melchisedech was, "without ancestry." We *do* move through solemn rites in a cloud of holy isolation. Our lives *are,* in purpose, plan, form, content, and function, as unlike the lives of laymen as a church is unlike their houses. For, by the priesthood conferred upon us, we are Other Christs, chosen by Him (though we wonder why) to be His "ambassadors," empowered by Him to be "the dispensers of His mysteries" of grace. Yet, beneath our august priesthood, beneath the image of the All-Holy Christ superimposed upon us, we are as human as anybody else. We hunger, we thirst, we grow weary, we take sick, we feel pain, we suffer temptations, we sin, we make mistakes, we fret under our incompetency, we know the meaning of discouragement and loneliness and boredom and frustration. Strange compounds we are, indeed, of so much that is of heaven and so much that is of earth.

Why do Catholics revere us? Not for our own sake, but for the sake of the Christ in us. With another priest, I once visited the home of a wealthy Catholic woman, in her sixties, known in her town as a world-traveller and an art-collector. We had hardly crossed her threshold till she insisted we *must* see a treasure she had discovered in Naples a month earlier. It was a fairly large ivory crucifix, exquisitely carved by an Italian Renaissance artist. She had hung it against a red velvet drape in her drawing room with a red-cushioned prie-dieu before it and a hidden light focused on it. "Isn't it perfectly *adorable,* Fathers?" she asked, pointing out the delicate detail-work, the crown of thorns, the drooping mouth, the contorted arm muscles, the nails, the wound in the side. "I'll confess, Fathers," she said, though not with confessional sorrow, "this is the first crucifix I have had in my home. I just couldn't *stand* disfiguring it with one of those common wooden or plaster-of-Paris things that clutter the American religious-goods market, with the *Christus* done so crudely that it's positively *revolting!* But this one"—she fixed a soulful gaze on it—"this one, well, I can kneel before this one and really *meditate!*" Father and I exchanged glances. I suppose we were both wondering whether in her alleged meditations the lady studied Christ Crucified or Italian Renaissance art.

Unlike that lady, you Sisters see and revere Christ in every crucifix, the crudest as well as the most artistic, the cheapest in material as well as the most costly. And, similarly, you see and revere Christ in any and every priest, the most worldly as well as the most ascetic, the most ignorant as well as the most learned, the most boorish as well as the most urbane. The Christ in one priest may be the resplendent Christ of Thabor: you honor that Christ. The Christ in another priest may be the bruised and bleeding Christ of Calvary: Him, too, you honor. With eyes of faith, so clearly did Saint Francis of Assisi discern Christ in all priests that he declared if ever he met together an angel and a priest, even an unworthy one, he would kneel down first before the priest. For a priest, he explained, can do what an angel cannot: he can summon the Incarnate Son of God back to earth in the Mass.

Now, after all this *Apologia pro Vita Nostra,* let's look at these "men in your life," the chaplains first. If you're ever stationed at your mother-house or your hospital or your orphanage, you'll probably have a resident chaplain. The odds are that he'll be infirm or old or both; otherwise the bishop would have him pruning vines and picking grapes out in the vineyard. He may be a cherubic old priest, gentle, genial, kindly, glad to do what he can for the Sisters, and thoroughly appreciative of what the Sisters do for him. If he's of that blessed mould, thank God and the bishop for him; and pray that he outlives Methuselah.

On the other hand, the chaplain may be a crabbed old priest, short-tempered, cynical, implacable; like the testy old chaplain at a mother-house who never tired of telling his clerical visitors, "Yes, yes, it's always the Right Reverend Mother and the Wrong Reverend Father!" Such a chaplain's motto is, "No frills!" This means, none of those Dialogue Masses and none of those feast-day High Masses and none of those novena prayers and none of those extra Benedictions. Distributing Holy Communion, he frequently barks, "Sister, open your mouth!" Try as she may, the Sister cook can serve him nothing over which he doesn't growl. He rages if a Sister, in an effort to turn chaos into cosmos, has touched anything on his desk. What can you do about him? Well, you can be grateful that at least he says daily Mass for you. Beyond that, give him the wide berth that he wants. And pray that his death, unlike his life, will be happy.

If you're ever stationed in a city convent, you may have a chaplain come to the convent for your daily Mass. You'll want Father to be prompt, and prompt he ought to be. But if once in a year he isn't, please don't rush immediately to the phone. The loudest alarm-clock, you know, can occasionally fail to alarm and city buses and subway trains can be held up by mishaps along the line. Allow Father a reasonable margin of time to get there—at least, twenty minutes—before you dial his residence. While you are waiting, why not anticipate some of the community prayers ordinarily said later in the day? From experience, I can assure you that Father, no matter how solidly the angels are on his side, will feel even unhappier than you when he walks belatedly into your sanctuary, conscious of some fifteen or twenty pairs of feminine eyes on him, and certain that few of them are alight with kindly empathy.

Then there are your pastors. The majority of those you deal with will be, I don't doubt, like your present pastor, priestly in all ways, devout, earnest, zealous, patient, selfless, considerate towards the Sisters, and appreciative of the Sisters' work and self-sacrifice. You'll find them almost always ready to cooperate with your suggestions regarding the needs of the convent or the school. In return, give them your own ready cooperation in their parochial projects whenever you can. The rectory-convent relations, after all, should be a two-way street, the pastor helpful to the Sisters, the Sisters helpful to the pastor. "Before all things," urges Saint Peter, have a constant *mutual* charity among yourselves . . ." (I Peter 4:8). (The italics are mine)

When your pastor, or any other priest, visits the convent, try to be friendly towards him, not merely respectful. Respect for priests, you know, doesn't call for a deep-freeze treatment of them, a prim, stiff, formal, self-conscious, aloof mode of behavior and speech that makes Father glance uneasily, like a little boy, to see if his fingernails are clean and his shoes shined. We priests like you Sisters to be relaxed in our presence; to act naturally, not preternaturally. We like you to talk with us freely, to jest with us if the spirit prompts you, to recognize our own pleasantries by a little more than a momentary flicker of a smile that religious decorum immediately jerks back under its control. And (may I say it?) we like you Sisters to let us visit your convent without your swishing off at once to the kitchen to get us lemonade and cookies, as though we had just been rescued after a foodless and drinkless week adrift at sea in a lifeboat. As the girth of many of us would suggest, we really *are* fed—and quite well—at our rectories and monasteries. We know, surely, that your intent is gracious, and that you're merely fulfilling a rite stressed in your novitiate days. But it's a rite the omission of which most of us will suffer gladly most of the time. Thank you, just the same.

But to return to pastors. Here and there, inevitably, you will have to work under one who is *sui generis:* like the Monsignor who, on March 17, picked up the sacristy phone, dialed the choirloft, and told the organist: "Professor, remember, I want 'The Rose of Tralee' played at the Offertory, soft and sweet, and 'The Wearing of the Green' at the end, full organ." The Sister sacristan gulped. She gulped again when the Monsignor turned to her and said, "None of these white vestments today, Sister. Get out the green."

"But, Monsignor," she faltered, "what about the rubrics?"

Tapping his expansive chest, he assured her smilingly, "I'm the rubrics around here, Sister!"

If a pastor insists on this kind of home-rule, you should politely protest against his arbitrariness, as did Sister; then, when your protests have been ruled out, you may, to avoid the greater scandal of pitched battle with him, give passive cooperation to his home-made rubrics. On July Fourth, let him wear a flag for a vestment if he wants to.

Or maybe a pastor makes unwarranted demands of the Sisters, for washing altar linens, sewing vestments, mimeographing bulletins, mailing raffle books, counting collections, typewriting reports, running a parish library, and the like. You, the Superior, must take a courteous but firm stand against all such supererogatory activities, or your Sisters will never know a free hour on Saturdays, Sundays, and holydays, including Christmas and Easter. Let Father enlist parishioners to do parish work. If he must, let him pay them out of the parish treasury. With all their work in the school and the convent, your Sisters, surely, are rendering the parish ample service.

Or perhaps somewhere you'll have a pastor who's an interloper, constantly cutting in on your school and your convent life. A Sister somewhere told me about such a pastor, and I'd never have believed her story if she herself hadn't been a part of it. This particular pastor was wont to eat his lunch sitting at the bay window of the rectory dining room, watching hawk-like the children playing in the adjoining school yard and the Sisters proctoring them. Frequently, if he thought the Sisters at all remiss in their supervision, he would bang a spoon or a fork on the window and point excitedly to some area of the yard that he thought out of control. Unheralded, he would burst into classrooms, make announcements, yank children out to run errands for him. At Sunday Mass, if the church was crowding, he'd bawl from the sacristy door, "Sisters, get up and give your pews to people who pay!" In his rectory office he had a microphone, connected to a loud-speaker in the convent; and whenever he felt the urge, even in the late watches of the night, he would blast notices to the Sisters: "Sisters—now hear this!" He made nervous wrecks of the nuns.

If, heaven forbid, you meet his counterpart anywhere (could there possibly be *two* of his kind?), you should report the wild state of affairs to your Major Superior. She, on her part, should serve the pastor an ultimatum, with specific demands concerning the Sisters' right to live and work unharassed. If the pastor doesn't comply with those demands, she should withdraw her Sisters from his school, even if he does happen to be a generous contributor to the motherhouse. The sanity of the Sisters rates top-priority consideration.

After chaplains and pastors, let us look at your convent confessors. Someone once asked the great Disraeli, Prime Minister of England at the time, what he looked for most in a member of Parliament. Disraeli answered unhesitatingly, "That he be there!" And that, surely, is the first requisite of the appointed convent confessor. After discussing the matter with him, agree on a set time for the weekly confessions, one that is convenient both for him and for all your Sisters. If Father is notably negligent in keeping his appointment, you should write a tactful letter to the Chancery ("It would appear that other duties have prevented Father, etc.") and ask for another confessor. Fear not: your letter won't be the first of its sort in the annals of the diocese.

Perhaps the confessor is no time-waster, like the legendary (and fictitious) confessor who streamlined the nuns' confessions to a seven-word formula: "Same as last week Sister? . . . Same penance." Or perhaps, if not a religious himself, he is prone to call "nonsense" such peccadilloes as the breaking of the Great Silence ("What's great about it?"), inward murmuring ("You mean a stomach rumble?"), impatience with school children ("I'd murder them!"). Gladly accept his absolution, but not his asceticism. These faults are the "seven-times-daily" faults of the just; slight, indeed, but still faults.

I want to remind you once more, dear Sister, that Canon Law prescribes that you must allow your Sisters to go out to another confessor whenever they request. They have the right, and you have the strict duty to honor it. Grant such permission graciously, with no temperature-taking looks, no questions asked. And here I remind you once more that you are strictly forbidden to demand of any of your subjects a "manifestation of conscience." Pope Leo XIII solemnly revoked, declared null and void, any contrary provision in any religious Constitutions. Canon Law echoes his prohibition. Should a Sister volunteer to manifest her conscience to you, you may allow her to do so. But since you are not a moral theologian, and are not expected to be, please do not attempt to solve a difficult case of conscience. Let a confessor do that.

We come now to your spiritual directors. Or do we? I mean, where are they? The spiritual books of earlier centuries are full of them, all right, and full of insistence on their indispensability. "Nobody," these books all sternly warn, "is a judge in his own case," or "He who has himself for teacher is the disciple of a fool." Yet for whom were those books written? For the main and mass of Catholics, the millions who had neither the money to buy a book nor the ability to read one? Was each supposed to have his own spiritual mentor? Or were those books written for the educated nobility, and particularly for the noble ladies, who sat in their castles with little to do but probe their psyches and discover spiritual complexes, neuroses, and psychoses all unknown to the Great Unwashed? Whatever the answer, many spiritual writers today put considerably less stress on spiritual direction. Some of them, like Moffat, Escribano, Granada, even question the need of it ordinarily.

The simple facts of the case, as I see them, are two: 1) On the American scene today, spiritual directors, outside of seminaries, are an almost extinct species. You are fortunate if you meet two of them in a lifetime. 2) Spiritual direction, essential in the beginnings of religious life and imparted usually in the novitiate, is not ordinarily necessary afterwards. Let me explain. Suppose that I'm driving along Route 1, which skirts the eastern coast from Maine to Florida. Beside me on the car seat I have an open road-map with Route 1 heavily pencilled. Every few miles I pass roadside signs that plainly say, black on white, "Route 1." I hardly need, then, to stop at every gas station and inquire anxiously, "Is this Route 1?" From at least one attendant I would probably get the answer, "Can't you read, Mister?" But if I come to a multiple intersection of roads, or if I have to make a detour, and afterwards I am not sure that I am back on Route 1, then I need direction and should ask for it, or I may lose time. Well, Route 1 is for us religious the Commandments, the Rule, and the Constitutions. If we keep to that route, what need have we of directions? But if we come to confusing crossroads or temporary detours, we need instructions from someone who knows the way. We need answers only if we have questions.

Who in such cases can and should direct you? Your regular confessor; he knows you best. And the proper place for such direction is ordinarily the confessional. (Some communities *insist* on this point.) You should rarely, if ever, seek spiritual direction, or permit any of your Sisters to seek it, by mail, and never by phone. Letters sometimes fall into the hands of strangers, and phone conversations are sometimes overheard along party lines. Maybe your previous confessor, now transferred elsewhere, *did* understand you so well; maybe, as Chaucer said of a friar, "sweet was his absolution." Well, he is gone now; and his successor, though perhaps less personable and less highly spiritual, has the same priestly powers that his predecessor had. The desire for special direction from a special priest is often, you know, nothing but a selfish seeking of special attention; the desire, Thomas Merton calls it, "to breathe a different atmosphere from the rest of men."

So much, then—or so little—about spiritual directors. Don't be aggrieved if you find none. Maybe you need none. Most of the greatest saints that I have read about had none either, except Teresa of Avila, who said her first one set her back about ten years. You have plentiful spiritual direction, I repeat, in your Rule and Constitutions and in good spiritual books, especially those written by saints.

Finally, we come to the retreat masters (he, one of them, said smiling). But what suggestions can I offer about *them?* Sisters invariably give their retreat master the reddest of red-carpet treatment. They receive him joyously, quarter him regally, feed him fabulously, hear him enthusiastically, thank him effusively. What more could mortal man want?

After introductory generalities, show him the tentative retreat schedule you've drawn up, and make changes in it that he might suggest from his experience, e.g., regarding the spacing of the conferences. But don't try to assign to him special conference topics ("They need a strong talk, Father, on sisterly charity"). Let the Holy Ghost take care of such matters. . . . See that in his room there's a Bible and a copy of your Rule and Constitutions and Book of Customs and a typewriter. . . . During his solitary confinement in the convent he will welcome the daily newspaper. . . . At the end of the retreat tell him that you liked his conferences, if you did; otherwise tell him that you thank him for the blessings he brought to your convent. In 1959, a Sister Superior assured a retreat master his retreat had been "the best ever." In 1960, writing to his Provincial for a retreat master, she added: "But please don't send us one like the one we had last year. He was a nice man, but he couldn't preach at all." She didn't know that the 1959 retreat master had been elected the 1960 Provincial. . . . The stipend for the retreat? There is usually no set offering. As pastors say preaching Christmas collections, "Give what you can."

A retreat is rightly called a time to be alone with God. For Sisters it is the only time of the year when this sort of solitude is possible. Let them alone with Him, then, most of the time; instead of bell-ringing them to the chapel every half-hour for the Rosary, the Stations, Litanies, or Spiritual Reading, as though they were high-schoolers who just *had* to be kept gregariously on the move or they would get individually into mischief. . . . Let them have access to a parlor for private conferences with the retreat master, if they want them. . . . Allow them time (the only possible time in the year) to "rest a while": with the rising time later than usual, and with time for an after-lunch siesta. . . . Pick a book of human interest for the table-reading, smile-provoking as well as thought-provoking. Or instead of table-reading, let them listen to some recorded spiritual conferences, a practice in many communities today.

Dear Sister, at long last I've done. I've done not only with this letter, but with all my letters on your role of Superiorship. And why have I talked about us priests in this last letter? Because I want my last word to beg your prayers for us. Some communities of nuns, you know, pray for nobody but priests. They know that a holy priesthood will mean a holy laity; that together the two will mean a holy Church. So, as you dearly love the Church, pray for us priests: especially for your chaplains, your pastors, your confessors, your directors, your retreat masters; not overlooking, of course,

Your affectionate uncle,

FATHER C.

Index

A NOTE ON THE TYPE

IN WHICH THIS BOOK IS SET

This book is set in Fairfield, a Linotype face, created by Rudolph Ruzicka, distinguished American artist and engraver. Introduced in 1940, Fairfield is almost strictly a book type with much charm and beauty. It is easy to read as one learns from extensive reading since it furnishes some degree of stimulation and pleasure to the eye. The fitting of each letter is practically perfect, which is a real tribute to its designer. This book was composed by Progressive Typographers, Inc., of York, Pa., printed by the Wickersham Printing Company of Lancaster, Pa. and bound by Moore and Company of Baltimore, Md. The typography and design by Howard N. King.